T0323180

NEW AND SELECTED POEMS

New and Selected Poems
1977–2022

ANDREW MOTION

faber

First published in 2023
by Faber & Faber Ltd
The Bindery, 51 Hatton Garden
London, EC1N 8HN

Typeset by Typo•glyphix, Burton-on-Trent DE14 3HE
Printed in the UK by TJ Books Ltd, Padstow, Cornwall

A CIP record for this book
is available from the British Library

ISBN 978-0-571-33855-9

10 9 8 7 6 5 4 3 2 1

for Alan Hollinghurst

Contents

2.

PART ONE

POEMS 1977–2015

I.

Anne Frank Huis

Even now, after twice her lifetime of grief
and anger in the very place, whoever comes
to climb these narrow stairs, discovers how
the bookcase slides aside, then walks through
shadow into sunlit rooms, can never help

but break her secrecy again. Just listening
is a kind of guilt: the Westerkirk repeats
itself outside, as if all time worked round
towards her fear, and made each stroke
die down on guarded streets. Imagine it –

four years of whispering, and loneliness,
and plotting, day by day, the Allied line
in Europe with a yellow chalk. What hope
she had for ordinary love and interest
survives her here, displayed above the bed

as pictures of her family; some actors;
fashions chosen by Princess Elizabeth.
And those who stoop to see them find
not only patience missing its reward,
but one enduring wish for chances

like my own: to leave as simply
as I do, and walk at ease
up dusty tree-lined avenues, or watch
a silent barge come clear of bridges
settling their reflections in the blue canal.

Serenade

There were the two ponies
and there was Serenade,
which belonged to my mother.
Though 'who belonged' would be better,
in view of the girlish head-lift she had,
and her flounce to and fro in the lumpy field,
and that big womanish rump I always gave a wide
    berth to.

When the blacksmith came to shoe her,
which was seldom in summer but otherwise often,
she would let him hoist and stretch out first one hind leg,
then the other,
with a definitely melancholy, embarrassed restraint.

The blacksmith was ferret-faced and rat-bodied,
hardly man enough to keep aloft the great weight
of one-foot-at-a-time,
although he did keep it sort of aloft,
crouched over double and bent at the knees,
to make a peculiar angle which held each hoof still
on his battle-scarred apron.

He would set up shop under the covered entrance-way
between our house and the stable block:
a ramshackle clapboard affair,
black, or black weathering to green,
with swallows' mud villages proliferating in the rafters.

I liked it there in the drive-through,
which was also where we parked the car
(but not on his days),
for the oil maps on the dusty cement
brilliant as the wet skin of a trout,
and for the puzzling swallow-shit patterns,
and most of all for that place by the corner drain
where a grass snake had appeared once,
an electric-green, sleepy-looking marvel
which, when it disappeared, left a print of itself
that stayed in the mind for ever.

The blacksmith always did cold shoeing,
prising off each thin moon crescent,
then carving the hoof with a bone-handled, long-
    bladed knife.

The miracle of no pain!
Serenade gone loose in her skin,
her strength out of her so she seemed suspended
    in water,
her hypnotised breathing steady,
the smell of piss, and musty hay, and ammonia sweat
    coming off her,
her head dropping down,
eyes half closed now,
and me a boy
watching the earth-stained sole of her hoof
turning pure white as the blacksmith pared
    and trimmed,
leaving the nervous diamond of the frog well alone
but showing me just by looking
how even to touch that,
much worse cut it,

would wake her
and break the spell
and our two heads with it.

Our collie dog sat near where the snake had been,
ravenous black and white,
all ears,
sometimes fidgeting her two slim front feet,
glancing away as if about to dash off,
then twisting back,
licking her lips and swallowing with a half-whine.

She knew better than to get under anyone's feet,
but when the blacksmith had done with his cutting,
and offered a new shoe,
and fiddled it downwards or sideways,
and hammered it with quick hits which drove the nail
    points clean through
(but these could be filed off later, and were) –
when this was all done,
he kicked the clippings across the cement
and now it was the collie's turn to show a sad restraint,
taking one delicate piece between her pink lips,
ashamed to be a slave of appetite,
and curving away into the yard
to eat it
in private.

The blacksmith straightened himself,
one hand smoothing the small of his back,
the other picking a few remaining nails
from between his own darker lips,
then slapped Serenade on the flank with his red palm,
rousing her from her trance,

running his fingers up her mane and over her ears,
giving each a soft tug and saying 'She'll do',
or 'Good lady', or 'There's a girl'.

Whereupon my mother herself appeared to pay him –
their hands met, and touched, and parted,
and something passed between them,
and the blacksmith took off his apron
with its colours of a battered tin bowl,
folded it,
and carried it before him in a lordly fashion,
using it as a cushion for his collapsed bag
of hammers, clippers, knives, files, pliers and nails
to the van
which he had parked in the lane some distance from us,
while my mother united the halter
and led her horse away.

There was a crisp clip-clop over the stable yard,
and a train of hoof prints with the neat shoes obvious
    to me,
who had stayed behind
with nothing better to do than look.

This was Serenade,
who would later throw my mother as they jumped out
    of a wood into sunlight,
and who,
taking all possible pains not to trample her down
or even touch her,
was nevertheless the means to an end,
which was death.

Now I am as old as my mother was then, at the time of
    her fall,
and I can see Serenade clearly in her own later life,
poor dumb creature nobody blamed,
or could easily like any more either,
which meant nobody came to talk to her much
in the spot she eventually found under the spiky may
    tree in the field,
and still less came to shoe her,
so her hooves grew long and crinkled round the edges
like wet cardboard (except they were hard)
while she just stood there,
not knowing what she had done,
or went off with her girlish flounce and
    conker-coloured arse,
waiting for something important to happen,
only nothing ever did,
beyond the next day and the next,
and one thing leading to another.

Kanpur

That light-sleeping night
slip-slap, slip-slap
was surely the watchman
about his business
in black marble halls.

Or was it the Ganges
compiling its sandbanks
just under our window
then sloshing them down
to a gluey green ripple?

No. It was the smack
of wet white plaster
dropped from the roof
on our separate beds
and the space between,

which showed next day
the dandering footprints
a lizard had scrawled
as it passed us by
without our knowledge.

Tamworth

Red brick on red brick.

A boiled eye in a greenhouse.

Lilac smoking in sere gutters and crevices.

A pigtailed head on lamp post after lamp post.

*

We had taken my mother's car
and driven into the blue –
she was in hospital then,
and didn't care.

*

Out of nowhere, nowhere else to go,
stuck in the dead afternoon, collapsed,

the mushroom hush of the lounge bar oozing up
through bilious carpet into our bed,

while men in the country nearby poked long rods
into voluptuous hedgerows, streams, rush-clumps,

fidgeting over the cracked hillsides shouting
Nothing here!, flinching at shadows, cursing.

*

We'd zig-zagged over the map
seeing cathedral cities –
any excuse had done
to get us a week alone.

That morning under Southwell's
swarthy prolific leaves
an imp on a fissure of oak
might have been Robin Hood.

*

It was not for us. It was death –
though the men came back empty-handed
and stacked their long poles in the yard.

They understood when we packed and paid.
There were other towns, sure – plenty,
if we could hurry – our last hour of day

squeezed by a storm from Nottingham way:
pitch, lemon-yellow, beech-green,
champing till ready, flighting a few big blobs

as the dusty country we entered
opened itself – leaf-hands splayed and grasping,
toads pushing up stones, mercury ponds blinking.

*

We'd kitted out the car
with a mattress in the back
and curtains made of T-shirts
exactly for nights like this.

Before we left the outskirts
we posted my mother a card,
knowing my father would read it
stooping above her bed:

Fantastic carving at Southwell!
The car's going a bomb!
Not one puncture yet!
The back's really comfy!

*

The thing we did – the thing anyone like us did –
was find ourselves lost and be glad of it,
chittering to and fro in a lane-labyrinth
with its centre a stubble bank at the head of a valley.

Therefore we went no further. Therefore we simply sat
and watched the sky perform: elephant clouds at first
with their distant wobble and bulge like ink underwater,
then splits of thunder, then sour flashes of light

glancing off metal, then clouds with hair clicked back,
edgy, crouching to spring, and when sprinting at last
fanned flat, guttering, flicking out ochre tongues
before losing their heads altogether, boiled down

to a Spanish skirt cartwheeling through woods,
a heavy boot squelching out squall after squall
of skin flakes, nail, hair, and Christ knows what
shrieks and imploring we never caught even a word of.

*

We burrowed against each other
after the storm had gone,
and saw between our curtains
lightning over the valley

on its nimble silver legs –
one minute round our car,
the next high up in heaven
kicking splinters off stars –

then skipping away to nowhere
with the thunder-dog behind it
grumbling but exhausted,
and leaving us such silence

I'd swear I heard the moon
creak as it entered the sky,
and the stubble field around us
breathing earth-smell through its bristles.

Belfast

I'm over to root up Larkin
but the ground is hard as stone.

His houses are both torn down.

His girlfriend has moved.

His writing paper is dust
lining a mouse's nest.

And the marvellous records which made him cry
are smashed and buried miles out of town
in that dump you pass on the airport road
where everyone's rubbish goes when they die.

               *

When I last flew away
I was home in time
to find you out.

You had taken your man
along the canal
where no one would see.

But I saw at once:
each eager hair
on his lanky head,

His yellow smile
which flicked like a fish
in stagnant reaches.

Yes I saw it all –
just from the way
two knives and forks

lay criss-crossed
on the draining board
in a crackling silence.

     *

That was another life.
But even in this one,
this new happy one,
it has taken less than a week
in a stripped-pine hotel
to be lonely as hell.

On the wet road below
a grey Land Rover woodlouse
gets a wide berth, and gives
a wild glimpse of soldiers
hunched behind bulletproof glass.
I was forgetting where I was!

     *

My taxi for Aldergrove
is cooling outside the bar
while the driver makes time
for talk and a quick jar:

Haven't found out much, then?
I dare say not.
At this late stage in history,
the past is one field of shite.

It's no good at any rate. No matter
how your man A loves your B
they forget them, or start
lying about them eventually.

You don't mind plain-speaking
do you? You do? Right; let's go.
What with Guy Fawkes and all
there'll be dire delays on the road.

Look

I pull back the curtain
and what do I see
but my wife on a sheet
and the screen beside her
showing our twins
out of their capsule
in mooning blue,
their dawdlers' legs
kicking through silence
enormously slowly,
while blotches beneath them
revolve like the earth
which will bring them to grief
or into their own.

I pull back the curtain
and what do I see
but my mother asleep,
or at least not awake,
and the sheet folded down
to show me her throat
with its wrinkled hole
and the tube inside
which leads to oxygen
stashed round her bed,
as though any day now
she might lift into space
and never return
to breathe our air.

I pull back the curtain
and what do I see
but the stars in the sky,
and their jittery light
stabbing through heaven
jabs me awake
from my dream that time
will last long enough
and let me die happy,
not yearning for more
like a man lost in space
might howl for the earth,
or a dog for the moon
with no reason at all.

A Blow to the Head

On the Metro,
two stops in from Charles de Gaulle,
somebody slapped my wife.

Just like that –
a gang of kids –
for moving her bag
from the seat to her lap:
a thunderclap
behind my back.

Very next thing
was reeling dark
and the kids outside
beside themselves:
You didn't see!
You didn't see!
It might be him!
It wasn't me!

For the rest,
she wept through every station into Paris,
her head on my shoulder like love at the start of its life.

*

By the merest chance
I had in mind
J. K. Stephen
who damaged his head
in Felixstowe (Suffolk)
in '86.

The nature of the accident is not certainly known;
in the Stephen family it was said he was struck
by some projection from a moving train.

Not a serious blow,
but it drove him mad
(molesting bread
with the point of a sword;

seized with genius –
painting all night),

and finally killed him
as well as his father,
who two years later
surrendered his heart
with a definite crack,
like a sla . . .

*

. . . which reminds me.
When I was a kid
a man called Morris
slapped my face
so crazily hard
he opened a room
inside my head

where plates of light
skittered and slid
and wouldn't quite
fit, as they were meant to,
together.

It felt like the way,
when you stand between mirrors,
the slab of your face
shoots backwards and forwards
with tiny delays,
so if you could only
keep everything still
and look to the end
of the sad succession,
time would run out
and you'd see yourself dead.

*

There is an attic flat
with views of lead
where moonlight rubs
its greasy cream,

and a serious bed
where now my wife
lies down at last
and curls asleep.

I fit myself
along her spine
but dare not touch
her breaking skull,

and find my mother
returns to me
as if she was climbing
out of a well:

ginger with bruises,
hair shaved off,
her spongy crown
is ripe with blood.

I cover my face
and remember a dog
in the reeking yard
when the kid I was

came up to talk.
I was holding a choc
in my folded fist
but the dog couldn't tell

and twitched away,
its snivelling whine
like human fear,
its threadbare head

too crankily sunk
to meet my eye
or see what I meant
by my opening hand.

Judgement

I was raking leaves in the front bed
when a helicopter wittered overhead

and I saw the blindness of a clear lake
when a waterbug paddles the far light.

My happiness went. I had thought of death
and everything that desecrates the earth.

I had watched the blood of my children spill,
and the stones crack open at my feet.

I had slithered so far into the underlying mud
I even flung out a hand for the hand of God.

  *

Other times
I am underground:
at dead of night
when green minutes
drip from the clock
and wear me down
to the sort of bone
a scavenger dog
picks out of muck
and buries later
but clean forgets,
so the years pass,
and the earth shifts,

and the bone turns
into nothing at all
like bone, or me,
or a single thing
waiting for light
and what it shows
of someone else
who lies awake
all night beside me
and never speaks.

*

For the first time in years
I am on my knees

in the sweet savour
of incense and soap.

The hand of God
is a burst of sun

torn through the head
of a window-saint;

the voice of God
is a fly in a web.

They are lost to me.
I shut my eyes

and imagine a bed
overlooking a garden:

knee-high grass
and hysterical roses.

The day is done
and there's mist coming on.

An apple tree
by the furthest hedge

has the look of my wife
when her back is turned

and her head in her hands.
The best thing on earth

is to call her and ask
for a drink of water.

I call and call:
the kitchen tap;

a drink of water;
a drink of water

to taste and be sure
I am dying at home.

Cutting

In a break for dreams
I glimpsed the bar
where I used to be young.

A '30s detective
was quizzing a local
in clouds of tobacco:

flecks of pewter
flew up the wall;
a horse-brass winked;

and there on my tongue
was your darkest secret
like Old Virginia.

   *

A hundred years old
at four in the morning
we clamber and slide
like seals on the ice.
Where am I now?

A senseless hand
is squeezing my heart;
a broken cry
has called us together
and will not die.

Then the ice flows collapse
and here comes the sea.
I am dead to the world.
It is all as I thought.
And who might you be?

*

Daylight falls
and my children trawl
the drizzling passage
from their room to mine
which takes them years
but is only a step.

Sunk on the bed
of a parched lake
where sleep ran out
I stare overhead
and brace myself
for their circle of eyes.

The time they arrive
is the time they go –
their almost inaudible
blobs of mouths
oooh-ing and aaah-ing
like shouting fish.

*We travelled for ever
to reach your door,
and in the end
we found it locked.
Wake up, damn you!
Wish us good luck.*

The Prague Milk Bottle

for Ivo Smoldas

The astrological clock
produces its twelve apostles
every hour

in a brainless, jerking parade
as windows wheeze open and shut,
Death twitches,

bells ping, and the cockerel crows
like a model train at a crossing
while I

get drunk in the sunlit quare with Ivo
surrounded by skirts as if nothing is wrong
except:

my bathplug won't fit the hole,
my water is cold,
my phone-call to home never works,
the exchange rate is fucked,

and the milk!

the milk of kindness, our mother's milk,
comes in a thing of French design,
looks like a condom and leaks like a sieve
and keeps us screaming most of the time.

*

In your wildest dreams you might whistle
and two ravens would flit their dark forest
for a baroque room you know is the British Embassy
(it has a view of Prague unmatched except by the Palace).

The ravens turn into girls and are painfully beautiful,
leaning with bare arms entwined,
black dresses crushed to the back of a yellow sofa,
to take in the city you never expected to see from
    this angle:

miraculous spires; ecstatic saints shattered by God;
and cobbled streets where the girls will squirm in
    your palm
then fold into wings and fly off with a gasp –
the sound of you waking alone in your dark hotel.

              *

It's not suppression,
it's humiliation.

The men they put in power
(they aren't stupid) – some of them
can hardly speak a sentence.

It's not suppression.
it's humiliation.

I have a headache. Nothing much,
but threatening to get worse – a tension
like the silence in a clock before it strikes.

It's not suppression,
it's humiliation.

My chemist writes prescriptions
but we have no drugs. I wish him ill.
None of this has much to do with girls.

                *

I leave Ivo to himself
and two hours later
he's outside at the airport
hoisting a bag
of toys for my children.

It's like seeing the ghost
of a friend whose death
made me say everything
there was to say.
Now there is nothing.

The milk of kindness
floods our eyes,
or maybe it's grit
swirled on the tarmac
in tottering cones.

We nod goodbye
where Security starts
and men in gloves
count my balls,
then I slither away

down a dingy tunnel
and turn again
to Ivo pinned
on a block of light
the size of a stamp,

his mechanical arm
glumly aloft,
his mouth ajar
to show he is screaming
if I could just hear.

Spring 1989

It is an Offence

The man in the flats opposite keeps a whippet
(once a racer) and two or three times a week
it craps by my front door – sloped, weary turds
like a single file of slugs in battle fatigues
(surprisingly slow for a whippet) – so that often
my shoes, my wife's, our children's bring it back home
to the stairs, the skirting, the carpets, the kitchen tiles
in bobbles, or flakes, or hanks, or outrageous
    slithery smears.

The sad old dog doesn't know what he's doing, and yet
I'd still like to cover his arsehole with quickset cement.

I admit that I also yearn to leave my mark on society
and not see machines or people trample it foolishly.

On the one hand it's only shit; on the other, shit's shit,
and what we desire in the world is less, not more of it.

A Glass of Wine

Exactly as the setting sun
clips the heel of the garden,

exactly as a pigeon
roosting tries to sing
and ends up moaning,

exactly as the ping
of someone's automatic car-lock
dies into a flock
of tiny echo aftershocks,

a shapely hand of cloud
emerges from the crowd
of airy nothing that the wind allowed
to tumble over us all day
and points the way

towards its own decay,
but not before
a final sunlight-shudder pours
away across our garden floor

so steadily, so slow,
it shows you everything you need to know
about this glass I'm holding out to you,

its white, unblinking eye
enough to bear the whole weight of the sky.

The Fox Provides for Himself

It could have been an afternoon at the end of our lives:
the children gone, the house quiet, and time our own.
Without a word, we stalled at a window looking down.

Weak winter sunlight sank through the beech tree
    next door,
skimming the top of our dividing wall, spilling a
    primrose stain
surprisingly far into our own patch. Earlier that
    same year

we had laid new grass, and the squares of earth
    underneath it all
still showed like the pavement of an abandoned town,
though the grass itself had done well, and from
    that angle

looked white as the breeze admired it, while we simply
went on standing there, holding hands now, trying
    to drown
the faint dynamo hum of London and lift off
    into nowhere.

Maybe we did drift a little. At any rate,
    something changed:
a shadow worked itself loose at the edge of our world.
Not a shadow. A fox. We saw it droop over the
    neighbouring wall

and step – using the sun as a plank of solid wood –
down through the air until, landing on all fours, it rolled
sideways (this was no stumble) and stretched out,
    owning the place.

Big for a fox, I thought, but said nothing, holding
    my breath,
the sun burning so far into his coat each bristle stood
distinct, ginger everywhere but in fact red rising
    through brown

to black, to grey at the tip, like bare plant stalks dying
towards the light, but of course soft, so I knew my hand
would come away warm if I touched and smelling
    of garlic.

First he just lay there, checking the silent earth with
    one ear,
but soon the music started and he was up – a puppet
living a secret life, stiff-spined but getting the hang of it,

doing everything he had seen real foxes do and not
    been able,
examining leaves, staring out flowers, then deciding to
    stop that,
there was no danger here, only pleasure, and to prove it
    he must

fold his dainty front paws, stick his ramrod brush in
    the air,
angle his plough-shaped mask to the grass, keep his
    back legs
normal, and shunt himself slowly forward inch by inch,

left cheek, then right, then left, then right again,
smearing his mouth so far open I saw the pegs
of his teeth – the pink inside the gums flecked
    with black –

before he tired of that too, and found under our
    laurel bush
the children's football, a sorry pink and blue
    punctured thing
which must be killed now, now, and in one
    particular way –

by flicking it smartly into the air and, as it fell,
butting it almost too far to reach but hoiking it back
on invisible strings, bringing death down in a frenzy

of grins and delirious yaps. After that, silence again.
When I returned to myself the fox was upright,
his coat convulsed in an all-over shrug

as if it were new and not fitting, like a dog when it jumps
out of water and stands, legs braced, in a halo of dew,
before trotting off in a hurry once more, which soon
    he did,

back to the neighbour's wall, and as he leaped he seemed
to hang on the bricks for a moment, slackened as though
his bones had slipped from his body, or so I thought,

watching the breeze re-open his fur, and waiting to see
how he dropped – hardly a fox now, more like a trickle
    of rust –
my hand holding yours as he went, then letting go.

The Sin

In the same moment I bent to the amazing
adder snoozing on the sandy path ahead,
the landowner was shouting from the sun.

What are you doing? I would have explained,
but one obvious reason had already gone
and there was no other. *Sir, not trespassing!*

A Fight in Poland

Beyond the outskirts of Gdansk
where the docklands and factories expire
in a shimmering wasteland
of foul-smelling marshes and greasy creeks,
and the Baltic chews over its sorrows
without attempting to resolve them,
I came to a hotel the size of a palace.

The lobby
had been decorated to resemble the interior of a gun case,
and was muffled with red velvet that a clever workman
had glued over mouldings and cornices;

my room
when I eventually found it after taking several wrong
    turns
along corridors where the floorboards groaned like
    prisoners
being tortured in a foreign language,
was simple as a hermit's cell,
with a window so gravely blinded by rain
I had to guess what lay beyond
was the dark brown Baltic shoreline.

I was already saturated.

I had no change of clothes.

But the bathroom shower worked after a fashion,
and an hour later I presented myself in the restaurant
where waiters slid smoothly between empty tables
while still managing to rattle the cutlery,
and shake a faint musical accompaniment
from the dry throats of wine glasses.

I ordered eel.
Six inches of shining green eel
and a bottle of white rioja,
which was enough to send me back upstairs
thinking I had drunk the electric Baltic
and was about to lose consciousness,
although I did have the presence of mind
to notice through a grille on the stairway
the sea still fizzing under its barrage of rain.

After a brief sleep or strong hallucination
I was woken by the sound of two men
fighting in the adjacent room.

Heavy, muscular men I could tell,
pounding each other with fists
in the stomach before taking a breather,
then resuming and heaving together on a bed
before tiring of that too
and, in the attempt to reach a conclusion,
throwing down onto the bare floor a mirror,
several books,
one glass followed by another,
and eventually toppling a wardrobe.

By that time I was used to the disturbance.
So much so, I even remained calm
when the door connecting their room to mine
bulged on its golden hinges,
debated whether to fly open,
then thought better of it and shrank back
into the flimsy boundary of its frame.

For this reason I said nothing next morning
when I took my place in the dining room
which I was glad to find now flooded with sunlight
streaming off the glassy Baltic.

And nothing again
when the waiter poured out my coffee
and the hotel slipped her moorings.

I expected my neighbours from the night before
would appear any minute beside my table
and either apologise
or wish me bon voyage,
but they must have disembarked already
and I soon forgot them.

I concentrated instead on the icebergs
as they sailed past my window.
The pale blue icebergs and the whales
that sometimes let fly with a waterspout
before they bent below the surface.

On the Balcony

The other, smaller islands we can see
by turning sideways on our balcony –

the bubble-pods and cones, the flecks of green,
the basalt-prongs, the moles, the lumpy chains –

were all volcanoes once, though none so tall
and full of rage for life as ours, which still

displays its flag of supple wind-stirred smoke
as proof that one day soon it will awake

again and wave its twizzle-stick of fire,
demolish woods, block roads, consume entire

communities with stinking lava-slews
which seem too prehistoric to be true

but are. Or will be. For today we sit
and feel what happiness the world permits.

The metal sun hangs still, its shadows fixed
and permanent. The sea-smell mixed

with thyme and oleander throws a drape
insidious as mist across the drop

of roofs and aerials, of jigsaw squares,
of terraced streets side-stepping to the shore,

or bathers sprawling on their stones, of waves
like other bathers turning in their graves,

and there, beyond them in the blistered shade
below the mountain, of the clumsy bird –

no, bi-plane, with a bucket slung beneath –
which sidles idly in to drench a wreath

of bush-fire in the fields, a fire that we
suppose means nothing to us here, but have to see.

A Dutch Interior

The dogs are a serious bore –
the pointer and the spaniel.
Their nails on the check floor
set painfully on edge
the teeth of each and everyone:
that stiffly standing page,

that dutiful and downcast girl,
and most of all that woman who
has recently uncurled
a message from its ribbon-ring,
read it twice, and now feels
all her strength departing.

A freshly whitewashed wall
behind her takes the weight;
stern morning sunlight pulls
her shadow to the dot of noon;
everything about her starts
then stops again.

The dogs, however, they
already know. See that one there,
the pointer? Just the way
he crouches shows he's lost the will
to fight. The path is clear
and sweetly open for the spaniel.

Bright Star

When I had walked the circumference of the volcano
and heard the pitiful groans rising from the crater
as well as that quick pattering sound like roof-tiles
shattering on a marble pavement, I caught the train
back to my apartment in town and opened a bottle.

The earth was beautiful then, and the heavens too –
so much so, I uncapped my telescope and let myself
prowl for a while across the milky ranges, descending
at length through the smooth branches of a lemon tree
to one especially bright star which on closer inspection
turned out to be a lamp blazing on my neighbour's terrace.

Of All the Birds

1.

Magpie

The magpie I like least
who stole my wedding ring
thinking it was his

to hide it in his nest
along with glass and pins
and other shining things.

2.

Nightingale

In the pine wood which grows on the sand dunes at
    Es Grau
rumour has it there are nightingales. Clematis we
    did find,

thick yellow and gold like honey turned back
    into flowers,
along with sea-holly, and lilies in their perpetual shade.

3.

Peewit

Eventually I decided on the field
planted with winter wheat, knowing
the farmer would crucify me if he saw.

It was all down to my kite needing
space not available in our valley,
although the ground was sodden,

and a trek to the centre hard-going.
A peewit kept me company, broken-
winged and weeping, *Over here!*

tempting me to some act of violence.
Never mind, as long as her plan saved
the nest with its clutch of speckled eggs.

4.

Dipper

One you showed me nested
on the far side of a waterfall,
another in what became a bubble
trapped when the current rose.

In all events the dipper marks
his passage with a flinty note
scraped against the softer sound
of everything that water says.

Then ups and quits his rock
to walk along the river bed,
as if a living soul had found
a way to haunt the dead.

5.

Cormorant

When it came to leaving
I went with the cormorant
flying well below the radar
and breasting the muddy lake.

Down the road was his double
at home on a rotting fence-post;
shabby wings hung out to dry
closed in the breeze of my passing.

Laying the Fire

I am downstairs early
looking for something to do
when I find my father on his knees
at the fireplace in the sitting-room
sweeping ash
from around and beneath the grate
with the soft brown hand-brush
he keeps especially for this.

Has he been here all night
waiting to catch me out?
So far as I can tell
I have done nothing wrong.

I think so again
when he calls my name
without turning round:
he must have seen me
with the eyes in the back of his head.

'What's the matter, old boy?
Couldn't sleep?'

His voice is kinder than I expect,
as though he suspects
we have in common a sadness
I do not feel yet.

I skate towards him in my grey socks
over the boards of the sitting-room,
negotiating the rugs
with their pattern of paisley dragons.

He still does not turn round.

He is concentrating now
on arranging a stack of kindling
on crumpled newspaper in the fire-basket,
pressing small lumps of coal
carefully between the sticks
as though he is decorating a cake.

Then he spurts a match,
and chucks it on any old how,
before spreading a fresh sheet of newspaper
over the whole mouth of the fireplace
to make the flames take hold.

Why this fresh sheet
does not also catch light
I cannot think.

The flames are very close.

I can see them
and hear them raging
through yesterday's cartoon of President Kennedy
and President Khrushchev
racing towards each other in their limousines
both shouting
I'm sure he's going to stop first!

But there's no need to worry.
Everything is just
as my father wants it to be,
and in due time,
when the fire is burning nicely,
he whisks the paper clear,
folds it under his arm,
and picks up the dustpan
with its debris of the night before.

Has he just spoken to me again?
I do not think so. I
do not know.
I was thinking how neat he is.
I was asking myself:
will I be like this? How will I manage?

After that he chooses a log
from the wicker wood-basket
to balance on the coals,
and stands to admire his handiwork.

When the time comes to follow him,
glide, glide over the polished floor,
he leads the way to the dustbins.

A breath of fine white ash
pours continuously over his shoulder
from the pan he carries before him
like a man bearing a gift
in a picture of a man bearing a gift.

Raven

Crashing the hush of winter and midday –
the fire ablaze but sunlight piling in
so flames look tissue or not there at all –
my father, in his Sunday best, appears
to interrupt me in the window-bay.
'What's this you're reading? Not the *Origin
of Species*?' I say, 'Hardly, Dad. It's *Calls
of British Birds*. You see? You want to hear?'

He settles down and I go mouthing off:
the barn owl's snore before its metal screech;
the starling's click; the jay's fantastic joke;
the robin's 'tic-tic-whee'; the raven's cough . . .
But then he's interrupting me again,
'The raven's cough? You mean the raven's croak.'

Passing On

By noon your breathing had changed from normal
to shallow and panicky. That's when the nurse said
Nearly there now, in the gentle voice of a parent
comforting a child used to failure, slipping her arms
beneath your shoulders to hoist you up the pillows,
then pressing a startling gauze pad under your jaw.

Nearly there now. The whole world seemed to agree –
as the late April sky deepened through the afternoon
into high August blue, the vapour trails of two planes
converged to sketch a cross on the brow of heaven.
My brother Kit and I kept our backs turned to that
except now and again. It was the room I wanted to see,

because it contained your last example of everything:
the broken metal window-catch that meant no fresh air;
your toothbrush standing to attention in its plastic mug;
the neutral pink walls flushed into definite pale red
by sunlight rejoicing in the flowering cherry outside;
your dressing-gown like a stranger within the wardrobe

eavesdropping. That should have been a sign to warn us,
but unhappiness made us brave, or do I mean cowardly,
and Kit and I talked as if we were already quite certain
you could no longer hear us, saying how easy you were
to love, but how difficult always to satisfy and relax –
how impossible to talk to, in fact, how expert with silence.

You breathed more easily by the time we were done,
although the thought you might have heard us after all,
and our words were settling into your soft brain like stones
into the bed of a stream – that made our own breathing
tighter. Then the nurse looked in: *Nothing will change
here for a while, boys*, and we ducked out like criminals.

I was ordering two large gins in the pub half a mile off
when my mobile rang. It was the hospital. You had died.
I put my drink down, then thought again and finished it.
Ten minutes later we were back at the door of your room
wondering whether to knock. Would everything we said
be written on your face, like the white cross on the heavens?

Of course not. It was written in us, where no one could find it
except ourselves. Your own face was wiped entirely clean –
and so, with your particular worries solved, and your sadness,
I could see more clearly than ever how like mine it was,
and therefore how my head will eventually look on the pillow
when the wall opens behind me, and I depart with my failings.

Are You There?

My father and I shove back the furniture
to the four walls of the sitting room
then lie on the carpet wearing blindfolds,
his left hand holding my left hand.

Well, are you there, Moriarty? he asks,
before tightening (I imagine) his grip
on his rolled-up copy of yesterday's *Times*.
There is only one possible answer to that.

I give it while rolling away to the side
but still clasping his hand, still in range,
and sure enough he manages a direct hit.
Now it is my turn, but the moment I lift

my weapon I realise there is no reason
to continue. I can tell from his silence
and the cold in his fingers, he was dead
long before he delivered the first blow.

The Mower

With storm-light in the east but no rain yet
I came in from mowing my square of lawn
and paused in the doorway to glance round
at my handiwork and feckless apple blossom

blurring those trim stripes and Hover-sweeps
I had meant to last. What I saw instead was you
in threadbare cords, catching the sunny interval
between showers, trundling the Ransome out

from its corner in the woodshed. The dizzy whiff
of elm chips and oil. Joke-shop spider-threads
greying the rubber handles. Gravel pips squeaking
as the roller squashed through the yard. Then a hush

like the pause before thunder while you performed
your ritual of muffled curses and forehead wipes,
your pessimistic tugs on the greasy starter cable,
more curses, more furious tugs, until at long last

the engine sulked, recovered, sighed a grey cloud
speckled with petrol-bits, and wobbled into a roar.
Off came the brake and off charged the machine,
dragging you down to the blazing Tree of Heaven

at the garden end, where the trick was to reverse
without stalling or scraping a hefty mud-crescent,
before you careered back towards Kit and me
at our place in the kitchen window out of your way.

To and fro, to and fro, to and fro, to and fro,
and each time a few feet more to the left, sometimes
lifting one hand in a hasty wave which said *Stay put!*
but also *I'm in charge!*, although we understood

from the way your whole body tilted lopsided
on the turn, this was less than a hundred per cent true.
Getting the job done was all we ever wanted,
parked with our cricket things and happy enough

to wait, since experience had taught us that after
you'd unhooked the big green metal grass-basket
with its peeling By Royal Appointment transfer,
lugged it off to the smoking heap by the compost,

thumped it empty, then reappeared to give us
the thumbs up, we were allowed to burst suddenly
out like dogs into the sweet air, measure the pitch
between our studious stump-plantings, toss to see

who went in first, then wait for you to turn up again
from the woodshed where you had taken five minutes
to switch the petrol off, and wipe the blades down,
and polish the grass basket although it never would

shine up much, being what you called venerable.
You always did come back, that was the thing.
As you also come back now in the week you died,
just missing the first thick gusts of rain and the last

of the giddy apple blossom falling into your footprints,
with bright grass-flecks on your shoes and trouser-legs,
carefree for the minute, and young, and fit for life,
but cutting clean through me then vanishing for good.

The Cinder Path

I know what it means
to choose the cinder path.

You might say death
but I prefer taking

pains with the world.
The signpost ahead

which bears no inscription.
The elm tree enduring

the terrible heat
of its oily green flame.

2.

from 'The Exploration of Space'

for Kyeong-Soo

Pyongsan

When you had scoured the bamboo clump and chosen
one stem suited to be the handle, you shredded the next
into shining strips to be the fist and fingers of the rake.

They scraped across the hillside making almost no sound
but a quiver like sound travelled continually up your arm
into your ear while bamboo leaves were scraped together
and others fell to muddle wherever your footprints went.

Kwangju

When I come to the border around midnight
holding your amazingly light body in my arms,
your feet kick suddenly and we cross over.

There is your grandmother walking ahead of us
along a narrow ridge between the paddy fields,
and kiss-kiss is the sound of her black sandals
making peace with the earth then taking leave of it.

Montauk

Remembering how a wave made in the Arctic
preserves its shape for many thousands of miles
provided the water is fathomless, and only starts

dying when the ocean bed shelves towards a beach,
whereupon the crest still travelling unhindered
gradually topples forward ahead of the toiling feet

with no choice except to disperse the energy it kept
so long in store, we caught the train out to Montauk
and were content all day to walk the windswept shore.

Orkney

We stopped for no particular reason I could see
beyond the bridge across a burn that hurtled
off the tops and into Harray's Loch. But doubling
back into the twilight of the arch where grass

had made a secret lip to catch the water's breath,
we found the otter's feasting stone beside the track
that ran between one disappearance and the next.

Home Farm

The hare we disturbed in the yard of Home Farm,
that either limped ahead of us or bounded or both,

paused whenever we at our dawdling pace dropped
out of view, and so seemed to be leading us onward

past the empty cattle pen and corrugated iron barn
stacked to the rafters with blue barrels of poison,

until we had reached the gateway and the grazing
where it turned for one last look, leaving us a view

of tall grass shining in the wind which was beautiful
enough but now hid something we thought we knew.

Holy Island

I am behind you on the mainland, leaning
on your shoulder and pointing with one arm
in front of your face at weightless cinders
which are ravens drifting above the island.

Boulder clay on the outcrops, and beaches
dotted and dashed with coal dust. Guillemots
whitening the cliff face. Small orchids clearly
still evolving in a downpour of cold sunlight.

How many years are there left to cross over
and show you things themselves, not my idea
of things? 25, if I live to the age of my father.
I cannot explain why I have left it as late as this.

Your black hair blows into my eyes, and I see
everything moving fast now. Weather polishes
the silver fields ahead. The ravens swoop down
and settle in the gorgeous pages of the gospels.

3.

from 'Laurels and Donkeys'

Setting the Scene

Before I come to the trenches, let me tell you the village
is a ruin and the church spire a stump; every single house
has been devastated by shell-bursts and machine-gun fire.

I saw a hare advance down the main street a moment ago,
then pause with the sun shining bright red through his ears.

Laurels and Donkeys

Afterwards, when everyone who suddenly burst out
singing has stopped again, Siegfried Sassoon settles
back into the haze of the old century. It is 1897, he is
11 years old, and this is Edingthorpe in north Norfolk.
His mother, wearing her light purple cloak, has packed
herself with the wicker picnic basket, bathing gear,
and three sons into the long shandrydan, drawn by a
donkey, which has been led round from the Rectory by
the gardener.

There is a plan to take a dip in the river but, as the
expedition begins, Emily Eyles appears on the doorstep
exclaiming Madam has left without her sunshade
after all. No matter. When everything is quiet again,
she closes it with a neat click and the faint creak of
collapsing silk, then traipses indoors where she falls to
thinking about Mr Dawson, her young man, who has
saved for long enough to open his shop in the village
when they are married next year. 'White wings that
never weary,' she sings, washing up cups and dishes.

By now the little party has reached the village church,
where Siegfried clambers down without the others
noticing, and leans his leather elbows on the lych-gate.
The carved gold lettering says it was built when the war
ended, in memory of a lance-corporal whose father was
rector here for 19 years and is buried nearby, although
the boy himself, having fought at Mons, Le Cateau, the
Arne, the Aisne, the First Battle of Ypres and at Hill 60,
drowned in the Transport *Royal Edward* crossing the

Aegean Sea on 13 August 1915. By peculiar chance it is
13 August today, and in a moment Siegfried's younger
brother will also be buried at sea, after receiving a
mortal wound on the Gallipoli Peninsula.

'Don't let the donkey eat the laurel!' their mother
tells the children; she knows it is poisonous. Laurels
and donkeys. Siegfried agrees but will not ruin his
afternoon, so picks a poppy and a cornflower, lays them
on the ground beside the lychgate, then turns placidly
down the farm lane, over the style, and along the path
that leads through the meadow to the Rectory garden
and so to the river, where in another short minute or
two the others will find him waiting.

The Life of Harry Patch

A curve is a straight line caught bending
and this one runs under the kitchen window
where the bright eyes of your mum and dad
might flash any minute and find you down
on all fours, stomach hard to the ground,
slinking along a furrow between the potatoes
and dead set on a prospect of rich pickings,
the good apple trees and plum trees and pears,
anything sweet and juicy you might now be
able to nibble round the back and leave
hanging as though nothing had touched it,
if only it were possible to stand upright
in so much clear light with those eyes
beady in the window and not catch a packet.

*

Patch, Harry Patch, that's a good name,
Shakespearean, it might be one of Hal's men
at Agincourt or not far off, although in fact
it starts life and belongs in Combe Down
with your dad's trade in the canary limestone
which turns to grey and hardens when it meets
the light, perfect for Regency Bath and you too
since no one these days thinks about the danger
of playing in quarries when the workmen leave,
not even of prodding and pelting with stones
the wasps' nests perched on serrated ledges
or dropped down in the caverns on thin stalks
although God knows it means having to shift
tout de suite and still get stung on arms and faces.

*

First, the hard facts of not wanting to fight,
and the kindness of deciding to wound men
in the legs but no higher unless needs must,
and the liking among comrades which is truly
as deep as love but without that particular name,
then Pilckem Ridge and Langemarck and across
the Steenbeek where none of the above can change
what comes next, which is a lad from A Company
shrapnel has ripped open from shoulder to waist
who begs you 'Shoot me, shoot me', but is good
as dead already, and whose final word is 'Mother',
which you only hear because you kneel a moment,
hold one finger of his hand, then remember orders
to keep pressing on, support the infantry ahead.

*

After the beautiful crowd to unveil the memorial
and no puff in the lungs to sing 'O Valiant Hearts'
or say aloud the names of friends and one cousin,
the butcher and chimney sweep, a farmer, a carpenter,
work comes to the Wills Tower in Bristol and there
thunderstorms are a danger, so bad that lightning
one day hammers Great George and knocks down
the foreman who can't use his hand three weeks
later as you recall, along with the way that strike
burned all trace of oxygen from the air, must have,
given the definite stink of sulphur and a second
or two later the shy wave of a breeze returning
along with rooftops below, and moss, and rain
fading the green Mendip Hills and blue Severn.

You grow a moustache, check the mirror, notice
you're forty years old, then next day shave it off,
check the mirror again and find you're seventy –
but life is like that now, suddenly and gradually
everyone you know dies and still comes to visit
or you head back to them, it's not clear which,
only where it happens: a safe bedroom upstairs
on the face of it, although when you sit up late
whispering with the other boys in the Lewis team,
smoking your pipe upside down to hide the glow,
and the nurses on night duty bring folded sheets
to store in the linen cupboard opposite, all it takes
is someone switching on the light – there is that flash,
or was until you said, and the staff blacked the window.

The Death of Harry Patch

When the next morning eventually breaks,
a young Captain climbs onto the fire step,
knocks ash from his pipe, then drops it
still warm into his pocket, checks his watch,
and places the whistle back between his lips.

At 06.00 hours precisely he gives the signal,
but today nothing that happens next happens
according to plan. A very long and gentle note
wanders away from him over the ruined ground
and hundreds of thousands of dead who lie there

immediately rise up, straightening their tunics
before falling in as they used to do, shoulder
to shoulder, eyes front. They have left a space
for the last recruit of all to join them: Harry Patch,
one hundred and eleven years old, but this is him

now, running quick-sharp along the duckboards.
When he has taken his place, and the whole company
are settled at last, their padre appears out of nowhere,
pausing a moment in front of each and every one
to slip a wafer of dry mud onto their tongues.

The Station at Vitebsk

Our town stood on the extreme edge of the world.
At the railway station, all the trains that drew up
to Platform One were returning home to Vitebsk,
and all the trains at Platform Two were departing

Vitebsk. We swung between hello and goodbye
like the long brass pendulum of the station clock
that never helped answer my question: were we
living near the beginning of time or the end of it?

The waiting-room had a ceiling painted blue and gold
but the atmosphere was always tense with anxiety –
everyone was preparing to leave for somewhere else.
They might hear the bell ring three times and still

have to watch their train disappear into the distance
without them: the destination had not been announced.
All they could do then was settle down to wait again,
as if next time the Messiah would finally show himself.

My beautiful train roared, the boiler gulped flames,
and steam swallowed truck after truck of passengers.
We were travelling at last, losing the town in a cloud.
I felt I might have been calming myself after a funeral,

or setting out on my way to a funeral. Would there be
a place for me when I arrived, and faces I recognised?
Would the trees still be there – the deep forest I knew,
and used to feel breathing on me when I was a child?

The Korean Memorial at Hiroshima

There was hardly time
between the Peace Museum
and the bullet train to Tokyo,
but our hosts instructed the taxi
to find the Memorial to the Koreans.
Ten thousand Koreans, killed that morning.
You, being Korean, had to see it.

* * *

We had been crying in the Museum:
the charred school uniforms;
the lunch-box with its meal of charcoal;
the shadow of a seated woman
printed on the steps of a bank.
Everyone else was crying too.
We shuffled round in a queue,
crying and saying nothing.

Then we stood in the rain
squaring up to the Memorial.
A spike of rusty flowers
and a tide-scum of dead cherry blossom.
Five or six miniature ceremonial costumes
made of folded paper and left to moulder.
Pink. Pink and custard yellow.
You could hardly leave soon enough.

* * *

The taxi only just made it,
sputtering among black cherries
then stalling by the skeleton
of the one dome to survive the blast.

No need to worry about the train, though.
The trains in Japan run on time.

In two hours and fifteen minutes
we would see Mount Fuji,
cloud-cover permitting,
and the snow-cap like a handkerchief
draped over a tumbler of water
in the moment of suspense
before a magician taps his wand
and the tumbler disappears.

Now Then

It was not my war, but all the same
my father handed over the harness
of his Sam Browne for me to polish,
and his enormous boots. There was
no way I could ever make the toes
brighter than they were already.

*

Years later I was riding a train south
from Gdansk to Warsaw at 4 a.m.
The pine forest swarmed beside me,
lit by the gentle glow of our carriages
and sometimes by devilish icy sparks
which flew from our wheels at points.

*

Tell him about the smell, my mother said,
working hard on his buttons with Brasso
at the window-end of the kitchen table.
She meant the smell of Belsen, the first
my father had known of any such place.
He slowly shook his head. *I don't think so.*

*

The forest lasted for miles. Miles and miles.
Then for a second I saw deep into the heart
of a clearing: there was this swineherd
lolling against the wall of his pine cabin
wearing the helmet of a German soldier.
And pigs rootling in the husky moonlight.

*

Why not? my mother continued her polishing.
Surely the boy is old enough to know history?
My father sighed: *Now then, you know the reason.*
That ended it. I kept my eyes down and attention
fixed on the long face looming in his toecaps,
convinced my efforts would never pass muster.

*

Eventually I slept, dreaming through what remained
of the great pine forest of Europe, while my father
pounded along in the dark outside my carriage.
At Warsaw he fell away from me, but not before
passing his boots through the window and asking
would I mind giving them a last quick once-over.

Demobbed

Sixty-odd years after the war ended my father returned.
No one had warned me to expect him, but long before
I reached the airport, crowds had already surrounded

the Arrivals Gate. When an especially loud cheer went up,
something told me it might be him, so I made an effort
to push through and enquire. Sure enough there he was

with his square shoulders, ramrod back and
    polished hair,
but wearing his city suit which surprised me, and at
    his side
my brother Kit. Kit obviously knew something I
    had missed.

In any case, they marched straight past me without
    so much
as blinking, while the crowd continued to cheer
    gratefully
and the brass band played 'Colonel Bogey', until
    my brother

wheeled aside and my father lowered his head
    to disappear
between those long yellow flaps that luggage
    goes through,
where I imagine he quite simply laid himself down
    and died.

The Minister

We flew Passenger to Kuwait,
where our driver ferried us to the military zone –
they were boiling tea at the checkpoint
and waved us straight through.

The Freight Building, next to Military Departures,
was signposted in Arabic script with a translation
that read 'The Fright Building'.

By the time our gate opened
I was weighed down by armour,
and accustomed to the American soldiers
who milled around us lazily
but always called me 'Sir'.

Our Minister, a late substitute and our *raison d'être*,
was another matter.
'Fuck this,' was his verdict on officials
who deemed our papers not in order,
and much else besides.

We wasted a day in the Meridian Hotel,
then next morning set off again for the airport.
The fourth approach road our driver tried
was the one without a blockade.
'Fuck that as well.'

The planes are in constant use,
so when our Hercules landed,
the pilot left the engines running
while the ramp
(which I recognised from shots of coffins coming home)
slowly lowered

and stopped 18 inches from the ground.
It was a struggle to get on board
what with my luggage and armour,
but I found my seat,
a narrow canvas bench,
next to a Major from 2 Para
who helped me with my belts and ear plugs.

There were no announcements.
We taxied,
roared down the runway,
and an hour later were in Basra
to take on an Iraqi general
and his American liaison officer.

Eventually we reached Baghdad and started to corkscrew,
dropping tin foil to confuse the heat-seeking SAM missiles
before making an exceedingly low landing.
When I jumped onto the tarmac,
it crossed my mind I might break something,
but I bounced and walked on.

Soon the Minister caught up:
What the fuck were we going to do now?
Why the fuck were we waiting in the open?
Where the fuck was the Puma
that would take us to the embassy?

'Look over there,' I said,
and a moment later we were lifting off again,
thrashing over the empty streets,
firing flares when the pilot received a message,
which turned out to be false,
that a missile had locked on to us,
and dipping close to the ground.

The roof tiles were wonderful,
but the Tigris a disappointing chalky brown.
The Minister certainly thought so.
'Looks like a fucking drain.'
The surface whipped into little peaks as we crossed,
and ahead lay our landing pad in the Green Zone.

We had arrived safely.
An hour later the Minister was in the bar
practising his billiards.
'Hi,' he said,
when I approached with our schedule of meetings.
'Finally we seem to have got our fucking passports
    stamped.'

Then he bent forward to concentrate on a difficult pot.

Losses

General Petraeus, when the death-count of
    American troops
in Iraq was close to 3,800, said 'The truth is you
    never do get
used to losses. There is a kind of bad news vessel
    with holes,

and sometimes it drains, then it fills up, then it
    empties again' –
leaving, in this particular case, the residue of a
    long story
involving one soldier who, in the course of his
    street patrol,

tweaked the antenna on the TV in a bar hoping
    for baseball,
but found instead the snowy picture of men in a
    circle talking,
all apparently angry and perhaps Jihadists. They
    turned out to be

reciting poetry. 'My life,' said the interpreter, 'is like a
    bag of flour
thrown through wind into empty thorn bushes'.
    Then 'No, no,' he said,
correcting himself. 'Like dust in the wind. Like a
    hopeless man.'

The Vallon Men

On the gently sloping hill behind Norton Manor barracks, home to 40 Commando, three trees, one for each marine, have already been dedicated to the memory of those killed

during their tour of Sangin in 2007–8. A week ago today, in bright November sunshine, fourteen more were planted to commemorate those killed during the last six months.

'It was a very hard tour,' said Gavin Taylor, aged twenty-eight and a father of three. 'We have lost a lot of friends. And we have seen a lot of things that are not ideal.'

Home Front

I knew we were in serious trouble
when I looked from the landing window
and saw the two of them together,
their hats showing above the front hedge.

Our boy saw as well and I called out:
'Don't let them in'.
But he thought it was Dad come back,
so ran downstairs
and when they knocked he opened anyway.

from 'Peace Talks'

1.

War Debts

I started living with Debbie when I was fifteen,
but I was never the best-behaved boy in school
so obviously she had a bit of a battle there.

Then I went to college but sacked that.

So my sister's boyfriend, he asked me
have you ever thought about joining the army,
and I told him I've not,
but I will now,
and next thing there I was
doing my Phase One at Pirbright,
then Larkhill – the rolling plains.

We knew, right, we knew we were going out,
and it was like,
guys,
this is going to be tough.

Did you know Camp Bastion is the size of Reading?
I didn't know,
and 95 degrees with your body armour.
One of my mates was hit there,
I say hit,
by a shower of Afghan fingers.

Friends at home can't understand what I'm saying.
It's the anticipation I'm used to.
It's the news I'm waiting to hear.
No rumours,
everyone quiet and waiting for the facts.

Surreal, if I'm honest, surreal when I get back:
the ease; the slow pace.
In Subway, for instance.
Cucumbers. Tomatoes.
You think:
Get it done *now*, so everyone can go!
Just come on!

Then you leave and roadworks are everywhere
with nothing moving and rain pattering
and clouds covering the stars.

The war debts will come out then.
You think:
my weapon, where is my weapon?
And you look for it.
You did everything with your weapon
and it's like
urgh.

You miss it.
Nobody understands but you miss it.
You took a shit with it.
You went running with it.
You did everything with it.

If you had a doss bag, you kept it close as you could,
or in your doss bag,
that sort of thing.

It's trust, you see,
you have to trust your weapon.
It's individual.

I'm Stephen North.
Lance Bombardier Stephen North.

2.

Fickelty

This time we were looking at transition, the next
    incarnation.
It's interesting. Soldiers carry a lot on their hats,
    you know,
and we talk together about sadness, the fickelty
    of mortality.

One man, he was always getting sand out of his nose
    and ears,
and as more sand came to him, more and more sand
    and dust,
he counted it; he knew how many grains of sand
    there were.

As for me, I read the Psalms. The Wilderness.
    The helplessness.
The rocks, stones, wind and thorn trees. I encountered
    them all.
But a dog collar? No. Collar crosses instead and a
    tactical flash.

Then I came home and here are my children and my
    little list:
roof needs fixing, grass wants a cut, the long
    green grass,
where's such and such for the kitchen, bathroom,
    everywhere,

and aaah I've wrapped the car round a tree, aaah. It's
    interesting.
Now I think we are beginning to see the bow-wave of
    trauma.
Therefore I go with the men sometimes, pray for them
    always.

3.

The Gardener
in memory of Captain Mark Evison

We spent
            many hours kneeling together in the garden
                                    so many hours
                        Mark
            liked lending a hand

watching *Gardeners' World*

building compost heaps

or the brick path with the cherry tree that grows over it now
            the white cherry
                        where I thought   I mustn't cry
                                    I must behave
        as if he's coming back

        *

It was just after Easter with everything in leaf
                        he is so sweet really
            but worldly
                        before his time

I kissed him and said
            see you
                        in six months   and he turned
        he turned and said

        *

I opened the garden for the first time
            the National Garden Scheme
                  you know
            what gardens are like in May
and this man was hovering around
            outside the front

as I walked down the side passage
      he said   I'm a Major
I said   Oh my son   he's in the army
      sort of brightly

            *

Then I was alone
            so I went   and I gardened all day

how slow   how satisfying

I felt next morning
            he was struggling for his life

            *

He would be home
                        with three transfers
            on three different planes

and if he died they would ring me
                        and they would go back
            and they would not keep coming

my daughter Elizabeth and I drove to Birmingham
        my mobile   there   on the dashboard

we had worked out the times of the last plane
        and we arrived
                        and he was still

        *

He was lying   he was
            with this
                        Mark
with this plastic sort of
                        bandage over a hole
        just like
                asleep

        *

The reindeer on TV   the wild reindeer
        giving birth in the snow
                with the rest of the herd scarpering

they have seen the eagle above them

but the mother stands still

what am I going to do   what

a bit restless   and everything
        but starting to lick her baby
                        with the eagle   watching

        *

I was thinking quietened   that is the best word
            I felt quietened
                        seeing the hills below
      as we came into Kabul

I was thinking   Mark lived in a very green place
            and here everything is purple
                  orange
                              Turner colours I call them

I was thinking   in my nightmares he is never dead
                  bandaged   lost   never dead
            with my love
                        circling
                  nowhere to go

I was thinking   thousands of lives in an instant
                              and the molecules starting again
            and the mountains never changing

I was thinking   how was I quietened
            how
                  but for a moment I was
            quietened
                  then losing height
      with the brown earth rushing to meet me.

The Fence

I found my way home but it was not until summer
ended that my mother brought herself to ask me
to make good the fence that marks our boundary.
I went out there with a box of nails and a hammer
and when a flock of crows in the trees surrounding
offered their comment, I remembered how the birds
living by Shamash Gate spoke in perfect harmony
with mortar shells falling. Then I began knocking
nails into the wood and everything near took fright –
although not my mother, who continued watching
from her chair on the porch. I have said nothing yet
of what it is like to reach the exact point where one
place become another, with no way forward or back,
and there is nothing else left to do except fall down.

Finis

My ancient lurcher knew me
    but he died.

My wife is still alive.

As for myself
    I lose by day the cup and frame
        of things I recognise.

At night my friends
    are hacked to death again
        and pieces of my mind
            break off and float away.

Just yesterday
    I lost the word
        for what is it that drives
            a boat along?

An oar.

In recompense
    my children ease my conscience
        yet their lives
            still drain the colour out of mine.

My other lines
    were meant to be a harness for the sun
        but I fell short
            and so they dwindled and became laments.

This is one.

4.

Mythology

31 August 1997

Earth's axle creaks; the year jolts on; the trees
begin to slip their brittle leaves, their flakes of rust;
and darkness takes the edge off daylight, not
because it wants to – never that. Because it must.

And you? Your life was not your own to keep
or lose. Beside the river, swerving underground,
the future tracked you, snapping at your heels:
Diana, breathless, hunted by your own quick hounds.

Self Help

for Richard Holmes

I set my course south-east, and go to find
the Margate where John Keats – audacious, well,
and braced to catch the moment that his mind
became itself – hired lodgings like the swell
he never was, just off the central square,
then take the narrow track through wheat fields on
towards the 'clift' (his word) and silence where
he saw Apollo step down from the sun.

I never got there. As I spun my way
through Kent, across the marches, fog rolled in
so fast and penny-brown I went astray.
A gauzy church came next. Some graves. And then
a man in irons crouching by a stone,
exhausted, bloody-faced, and not alone.

The Realms of Gold

In a quiet part of Leamington Spa,
in the same flat
where he has lived all his life,
sixty-two-year-old Michael Standage
is close to completing his biography
of the poet D. J. Enright.

Nobody reads Enright now
apart from a few surviving friends,
and a handful of fans
who insist he is underrated.

Standage does not speak to them.

He is nervous of an interpretation
that differs from his own,
and they are jealous of him;
it's not as though his book
is authorised or anything;
he just got there first
and found that archive in Japan.

All the same, Standage
is confident of a clear run home.
He works late each night,
and only pauses
to watch a black wind stirring the trees
that line his side street but stop
where it meets the main road.

*

Meanwhile the poems of D. J. Enright
gather dust in second-hand bookshops
or fly into a skip
with other unwanted things
that go when a life ends.

A long history of adventure and homecoming.

A fastidious editor yet free
to travel in the realms of gold.

A highly original mind
with Proust among others
virtually off by heart.

And speaking of the heart . . .

But to date only Standage can do that
with any confidence.

The rest of us, the few
of us,
open the dark green *Collected* and think:
this was a life as good as any;
who am I to let it vanish completely
without returning an echo?
When I read him and I listen
to the silence following,
I know
exactly what he means.

*

Standage makes an exception to his rule
and accepts my invitation to meet.

We decide on Brighton,
which is neutral ground,
and walk for an hour on the shingle.

Following publication
can we look forward
to a revival of Enright's fortunes?

We both sincerely hope so,
and while the dry grey stones
grind under our shoes,
extol the virtues for which we feel
a common admiration,
especially as they appear
in *Paradise Illustrated*
and *The Terrible Shears*.

Once we have reached our climax
we stand precisely still
and stare across the sea.

Small waves beat towards us,
fold over neatly, and crumble into foam.

Very soon more follow and
the same thing happens.

London Plane

They felled the plane that broke the pavement slabs.
My next-door neighbour worried for his house.
He said the roots had cracked his bedroom wall.
The Council sent tree-surgeons and he watched.
A thin man in the heat without a shirt.
They started at the top and then worked down.
It took all day with one hour free for lunch.
The trunk was carted off in useful logs.

The stump remained for two weeks after that.
A wren sat on it once.
Then back the tree men came with their machine.
They chomped the stump and left the square of mud.
All afternoon the street was strewn with bits.
That night the wind got up and blew it bare.

The Customs House

I kept to backroads on my way to the Customs House
but now I have arrived it is impossible to travel further
without paying export duty on the merchandise I carry.

They have torn down the old buildings and laid new grass
so the officers can see me approaching without difficulty
and prepare their long form with its infuriating questions.

Beyond them efficient-looking factories and a white church
inside a white wall are almost drowning in torrential leaves.
A jungle! I imagine dangerous animals might well live there

until I notice a man emerging with no obvious signs of fear.
He seems to be dragging a cart containing a chest-of-drawers.
If he were in my position, he would pay very heavily for that.

Whale Music

In the beginning I found it difficult to believe
I was in fact alive. Was I a creature or a country?
I decided creature, and at the same moment also

discovered my voice. It was not so much a form
of communication with others as a way of proving
I was alone in the world, which has remained true.

Nevertheless, I continue to announce my presence,
speaking in tongues that create a definite shape
for everything I see, which is a glassy universe

without borders, crossing-points or territories,
let alone walls or doors, light or dark. Only currents,
fluctuations of temperature that mean almost nothing,

and sometimes, if I surface, the moon- or sun-light
in which I cannot fail to notice that by living slowly
I have become a catastrophic danger to myself.

                    *

When we abandoned our lives as gods or curiosities
we neglected to develop a sufficient appetite for safety.
The times you dashed at us with boats and harpoons

we might have dived down out of range but instead
stayed in clear sight and died. You could say therefore
the impression of wisdom given by my colossal forehead

is a complete illusion – although as we gathered together
making only confused and feeble attempts to flee
we proved something you are still failing to understand.

*

I can confidently say I was never more amazed by my
     own size
than the day Brendan the Navigator and his flock
     of monks
managed a landing on my back in the midst of their
     isolation.

Presuming me to be an island, they then lit a fire of
     driftwood
and said Mass in thanks for their Salvation. In their
     sleep later
I ferried them to shallow water, where in time they
     went ashore.

*

When first recorded by listening devices my voice
was understood to be the ocean floor creaking
which is a means of calling it the loudest sound

of any creature that has passed through the world.
Other impressions I give include gentle clicks;
a squeak like an immense underwater prison door;

clangs like the same door slammed hard shut
every seven seconds; and Morse code suggesting
human talk. This is the most recognisable sound

to you, and also the most mysterious since it allows
a perfectly good idea of what it is you want from me,
although how you might reply you know less well.

*

Now she is long gone I can only speculate
and make that my existence. I heard her speak
once, a pressure through water like a wave

inside a wave, but I never set eyes upon her.
The green chambers of my interminable palace
were deserted – emptiness succeeding emptiness.

It was the same when I dived down to the depths.
Was she there? Not so far as even I could make out.
The life I have without her is apparently complete

and doomed, but I deny this has made me a failure.
Like her, I am a prisoner of the splendour and travail
of the earth, but grateful to prove I have existed at all.

*

I have given you many long and tall stories to complete;
millions of soft lights; an excellent means of lubrication
for watches and other fine instruments; delicate bones

for corsets and strong ones for decoration and building;
the good edible meat of my body; and not to be
    forgotten
ambergris – which one scientist has said reminded him

of 'An English wood in spring, and the scent when you tear
back the moss and discover the cool dark soil underneath'.
My last gift of all will be the silence of your own creation.

The Conclusion of Joseph Turrill

Garsington, Oxfordshire, 1867

I was cut out for a quiet life.
Whether I have managed any such thing
is another matter,
what with larks to shoot,
and harvesting, gooseberries and whatnot.

Then there was all that with Netty.
Would she or wouldn't she?
Did I or didn't I?
It is my belief
I spent more hours kicking my heels at the gate
than happy the other side.

Be that as it may.
Anno Domini drives out matters of fact,
and faults that appear to us
when we compare the lives we have
to those we imagine . . .
There's nothing a gentle stroll
in the woods by moonlight can't put right.

I tried that just now.
I saw swallows on the branches likes clothes pegs,
which put me in such good humour
I brought home one of their nests and also four chicks.

The Discoveries of Geography

From day one I started to embroider,
and in no time was suggesting a country
far to the North,
where fish are as large as dragons,
and even minor administrators
eat off gold plates
and sleep on gold beds.

This is why I have packed in my birch canoe
a robe
made of the feathers of more than a hundred different
    species of bird.

So that when I have finally crossed the Ocean
I will have a ceremonial costume
rich enough
to impress in my encounter with the Great Khan.

*

We have an excellent long boat with outriggers
and therefore travel dozens of miles in a day.

Furthermore, and speaking as a navigator,
I can predict every fickleness of weather
and also the change in direction of currents,
sometimes dipping my elbow into the water
and sometimes my scrotum
to feel the slightest change in temperature.

These are the reasons
I shall be considered a saviour by my people
and die in peace.

In my own mind I am a simple man
who threw his spear at the stars
and landed there himself.

                *

I now have in my possession a map:
two handfuls of mud
scraped from the bank of our sacred river,
flattened into a tablet,
baked,
then pierced with the blunt point of my compass
while I spun the other, sharper leg
to produce the edge of the world as I knew it,

and beyond,
the salt sea on which I am perfectly at home.

In this way I look down at myself.

I think: I am here.

                *

Astonishing how many horizons are open to me:

at one time mountainous heaps of smashed slate,

at others a vast delta of green and crimson light.

And every day a different shore-line ripples past
bearing its cargo of white sand and dark palms.

Very beguiling they appear, but all encumbered.
All spoiled by the tantrums of their local gods.

Out here there are storms too,
but in the religion I have now devised for myself
I am convinced
the shaping hands have pulled away from us at last,
so the earth hangs with no support at the centre of –
what?
That is the question I have in mind to answer.

     *

You might suppose better charts would help me,
but in spite of their much greater accuracy
in terms of coastlines and interiors,

and the intricate detail
guaranteed by developments in printing,

not to mention the understanding of perspective,

empires still lie about their extent and stability.

These are the simple deceptions.

More difficult,
as I continue North to my final encounter,
and wave-crests flicking my face grow colder,
and daylight a more persistently dull dove-grey,
is how to manage my desire to live in the present
for all eternity,
as though I had never left my home.

*

It transpires the last part of my journey
requires me to abandon everything I once knew,
even the gorgeous costume
made of the feathers of more than a hundred different
    species of bird.

No matter, though.
It is delicious among the constellations,
as the planets begin to display their gas-clouds
and the beautiful nebulae their first attempts at stars.

When I look over my shoulder
to see my own blue eye staring back at me,
I realise before I disappear
I still accept what it means to be lost.

Hosannah

A donkey sharing its stony field with a Nissan
somebody dumped years ago in the top corner
is still curious how this came to pass. As his lips
browse the cracked bonnet, and his weeping eyes

take in the long arm of a fig tree with many elbows
stretched across both front seats, a great multitude
of mosquitoes sways above the hollow of his back
acknowledging silence first one side then the other.

The Death of Francesco Borromini

for Peter Maxwell Davies

The architect Borromini, born Francesco Castelli
in Bissone on the shore of Lake Lugano in 1599,
is dying by his own hand in Rome as evening falls
on 2 August 1667. The point of his sword has narrowly
missed his heart, which by good luck or bad judgement
means he has time to summon a priest and confess,
also to recall what he must leave behind in the world.
To the confessor he freely admits it was impatience
at not having a candle to continue working in the dark
that persuaded him to place the sword against his chest
and fall upon it. Meanwhile in S. Carlino, his earliest
and still-unfinished masterpiece, the last sunlight burns
down through the eye of the dome like an angel arriving
to ask of those within: *Which of you has been my servant?*

*

In the hollow earth beneath S. Giovanni dei Fiorentini
a crypt as immaculate as a blown egg is the setting
for the most intimate and intense theatre of his death
and life. Someone, an already grief-stricken friend,
has left a pair of women's ballet shoes by the altar,
setting them neatly side by side and then departing.
The suggestion is that whoever it was understands
the weight of stone is the same as the weight of air
and, like a breeze blowing across a field of wheat,
will sway, curve, vault, bow, spin, stop and stand
with a visible force and leave the clear impression
of things by nature continually unseen and invisible,
or like a dancer, their white shoes printing the stage,
pounding it, even, but only to leap upwards and vanish.

S. Giovanni in Laterano is the next place of pilgrimage
for his dying mind on its final inspection of everywhere
that proves the thing it was. Medieval brick cries out
beneath the new, austerely swaggering stone: *Mother
and head of all churches in the city and upon earth.*
Echoes crumple into the bays; they rise and multiply
under the glamorous roof; they glide over the tombs
where death is already ensconced and grinning. Each one
is pitch perfect. It is like watching a parliament of crows
at sunset, when the whole sky darkens with their arrival
and, above and beyond their big racket of conversation,
creaking wing feathers take complete control of the air
as many thousands of birds swoop into their own places,
where in a second they fall silent and will suddenly sleep.

*

Now it is the turn of the tongue, wondering how to speak
at last of S. Ivo alla Sapienza, the old university church,
where six bays represent the body, head and four wings
of the bee, which symbolises the Barberini family, but also
the star of David, since the significance of stone continually
shifts its ground without moving. By much the same means
the confusion of Babel tongues blathering all over the tower
might also be a sign of wisdom, the gift of tongues, in fact;
or the very form of the vault – an immense marquee of light –
could be persuaded to reappear in a small tent-like silk cover
placed daintily over the tabernacle containing the sacrament.
There, the tongue wants to say and the brain too: *the meaning
of this is definitely that.* Then the incandescent brass bell tolls:
Never one thing. Never one thing. Never one thing. Never one.

*

In a glimpse of the afterlife, Borromini now claps his eyes
on the leading twentieth-century interpreter of his work,
the university professor, Surveyor of the Queen's Pictures,
Director of the Courtauld Institute and Communist spy
Anthony Blunt, climbing back stairs with special permission
to reach the roof of the Palazzo Falconieri. Here he finds
something not easily seen at street level: a concave loggia
crowned by a balustrade carrying Janus herms, whose two
faces in each case make a striking silhouette against the
      sky.
One looks over the tangle and rumpus of the city; the other
across the Tiber to Trastevere. As soon as the difference
is clear, all eyes that can turn now look in the same
      direction,
to see the long river carry away everything it still reflects
over the raking weirs and beneath a succession of bridges.

          *

The last light is still sliding in a single weak column
through the dome of S. Carlino where he observed it
in the beginning, inscribed with fine curlicues of dust.
Borromini lies down and places his right eye exactly
under the beam, so it becomes a telescope to heaven –
except he is looking through the wrong end, and sees
only his young self setting out, complete with a plan
that matches his delirious heart to his meticulous brain.
There is no mistaking the brilliance of this, or the damage
he will do to himself. Jealousy and hypochondria. Rage.
Genius and more rage. Then the light disappears entirely.
With the sword run through my body I began to scream,
and so they pulled the sword out of my side and put me
here on my bed; and this is how I came to be wounded.

PART TWO

POEMS 2015–2022

I.

from 'Essex Clay'

Juliet

1.

The intact frost of early morning
    and a blade of ice
        drawn from the tap in the stable yard.

The village as they drive through
    half asleep under twisting chimneys.

The church   Victorian Doomsday
    moored to the hilltop
        with its pretty flotilla of graves.

The weathervane cockerel's gold and flying eye.

The lane
    straightening beside water meadows
        its thatch of bare chestnuts
            shattered with daylight.

Gravel in the ford
        washed by the brimming stream
    the Blackwater
and pebbles magnified   tawny   beach colours
    with that other river   the river of shining tar
    shivering below.

Last night's snow dust
        in suddenly wide-open ploughed fields.

Flints like hip bones and knee bones.

Clay clods supporting
        miniature drift-triangles on their windward side.

His mother beside him
        yellow hair trapped and placid in a hairnet
clean cream jodhpurs   red collar   black riding jacket
        stock like a bandage
                gold pin
                        adorned with the mask of a fox.

                *

He is seventeen   confident   opinionated
        and definitely at odds
                on this subject at least.

He does not approve.

But when he glances into the footwell
        and sees his mother's narrow feet
                fluffy sheepskin slippers
                peddling by turns at the brake
                        accelerator   clutch
        he is silent.

He cannot bring himself
        to make that scene again.

                *

In the car park of the White Hart
    also the bus stop
        he condescends   tips his head a little
    kisses his mother goodbye
        a skim of skin
        is enough
but catches still in close-up her hairnet
    a black cobweb   tougher of course
        and feels it
          scratch
            the tip of his nose.

Then he is busily out in the wind buttoning his overcoat
    the ankle-length   topsoil brown   soldier's greatcoat
    the British Warm
        borrowed from his father without permission
    stolen more like
which makes him   he thinks   beside his holdall
    soldierly after a fashion.

    *

Exactly as his mother grinds the Hillman into gear
    the silhouette of his bus
        bulges over the hilltop beyond the White Hart.

He flinches away
    to discover his mother's face is already no longer her face
        but an after-image
        hovering a little way behind her
as she guns the engine   and wriggles into the traffic
    flow.

Her exhaust plume rapidly fades into the spectre of
a spectre.

Dark petrol specks escaping the pipe
    might well be a trail of breadcrumbs
        dot-dot-dot all the way home.

And the bus
    the snow-filthy bulk of it
                amazingly
            stops
    when all he does is hoist his arm.

    *

From the front seat on the top deck
    smearing window-fug
        with the whiskery coat sleeve that makes an O
    fringed with delicate scratch marks
he can pretend the world is simply a cabbage field
    creased with snow.

And there is no one the entire journey
    even to notice   let alone ridicule
        either the relief or the alarm of solitude
            he reveals
by leaning his head against the glass
        on the trembling chill
            and pretending he is asleep.

Although despite appearances
    he is still watching in fact
        the shadow of the bus shrink
            where it meets a burst of heavy snow
        then elongate as the snow weakens

while he also imagines
        clay six feet deep
                the malevolent pasty glue
                        the ash smears and ochre
                waiting with all the time in the world
        to sculpt its lead around gumboots and plough blades

to rear and obliterate whatever it can

until an hour has gone
                and the bus flusters into Sawbridgeworth
                        where its shadow abruptly
        concertinas in through the window and sinks down
                among the other shadows already assembled
                        and is absorbed.

        *

Clambering out
                holdall thumping the door
        he forgets himself the instant he sets eyes on her.

Juliet.

Her face and playful love-name coinciding.

Her black hair   black
        not a black enough word.

Her red mouth.

Her skin white   but mainly full
                ripeness.

Her eyes liquid pouring
    straight into him
        her eyes glittering and
            completely ignoring her mother
    which he should not
    so he shakes her mother's hand.

Headscarf   specs   face-fuzz powder
    how was your journey
        her space-voice dustily tinkling far elsewhere
    with Juliet continually here-and-now.

    *

His cheek brush-collides with her cheek
    and he smells   peppermint
        should have thought of that.

Never mind.

Just find the car and
    but
        wait
    front seat or back.

Back.

Then ok hunch forward laying one forearm flat
        on pale green clammy plastic
    apparently all relaxed like
    despite Juliet's black hair a swelling wave
trapped inside her collar.

And breathe
        is the cliché
                he cannot resist.

And keep
        breathing.

Until they set off and shops   shop-fronts   shoppers
                distract him
        and the heater cranks up
                and mist solidifies into dribbles on the windscreen
                        and Juliet
                        summons him
        simply by wriggling her hand
                inside this wave of black to set it free
                        so it flood-slithers
        over the shoulders of her coat onto his hand
which jolts in the electric shock.

        *

Afternoon already somehow
        and despite the cold
                clouds and snow shovelling in west from Siberia
                        he and Juliet leave her house for a walk.

He spares a thought for his mother   wondering
        will she be home already
                defeated
                        she would say that
                defeated by cold.

But the thought vanishes
        when they step from the lee of the house
                and ice puffs immediately slit his eyes
        confronting a dead prairie sprinkled with snow
            stones
                    his greatcoat not so ridiculous now
no more at least than Juliet's white fur hat
        and Doctor Zhivago number
                fur blustering at collar and wrists
        while she butts into the wind
                    one blue vein pulsing in her porcelain neck.

            *

Down the long narrow headland they go
        snowflakes sugary on winter wheat dithering
            beside them.

Jesus though it is laughable this cold
        laughable and
                gets the better of him
                rotating him
                veering him back the way they came
        only to find Juliet
                akimbo in his way.

His eyes
        blur in the windswept peering.

His heart
        starfish
                touches all four walls
                        ceiling and floor
        of his rubbery chest cave.

His hand
        animaly inside her coat
                scalds on astounding radiator heat
                        when he touches bare skin
                between the waist of her jeans and her jersey.

And her mouth
        her mouth gasps into his ear
                the blaze of his own name.

        *

But first the party   they did give their word
        and Juliet
                despite his flagrant stare
                        to show how much he would rather not
despite her own luxurious deep mermaid curl
        in the wave of an armchair
                left hand   square-tipped fingers
                        tightening round her bare ankle
                and the little vein mesh there
        the blood delta
                pale lavender
Juliet is determined they should keep it.

        *

So he collects and removes himself
        as ordered into the soft-lit
                oak-panelled spare room
                        with its cosily low ceiling.

He takes time
        shaking out creases
                from his brand new white shirt
                        with risky jabot collar
        his father would not be seen dead in.

He sounds
        with all he dare of his weight
                the nervous springs in the high bed.

He begins to imagine later
        or will it be her room.

        *

But a knock interrupts him
        the polite wood-knuckle sort.

Juliet   he thinks
        has she   what
                is she
        here now already.

Then the door creaks and not Juliet
        Juliet's mother
                stares in.

His smile stiffens.

He asks himself   has she spied in his head
        and seen their plan laid bare.

But no.

Spying would not explain why
        she is pinching her nose
                dimpling the eiderdown with her fingertips
                        the silver blue eiderdown
        stitched into lumpy waves
to occupy herself with the pattern she makes.

        *

A grown woman she is obviously
        with her whole face crying
                like suffocation.

A face doing its best to look up
        still crying
                then methodical   for a moment at least

                his father
                has called
                on the telephone
                and his mother.

        *

But now it is his turn to interrupt
        his turn
                to take pity and
                        with the inspiration of dread
with a mind-burst like a sapling instantly becoming a tree
        tell her   he knows already
                        what she is about to say.

Adding to himself at least
        he has expected this
                all his life
            and is Juliet   where
                waiting
        or not any more
                    how could she be waiting
or him
        how could he still be waiting
                    not after this.

                *

In the pause following he sneaks
        a look into the future   thinking
                he can beat facts at their own game.

He sees his mother on a high pillow bank
        yellow hair no
                shaved hair no   brush-bristles
                    no longer summery fair.

Succulent bruise red green grey
        maturing into a dead colour already
                moleskin.

Beautiful thinness
        bloating into a big belly
            a flagon
        pumped with drugs through a murky tube
                darting into the crook of her elbow.

Eyes dusty   eyes shut   eyes
      for three years
            he cannot yet
                  count exactly cannot

      bring himself to that horizon
            eyes sunk into eye sockets unconscious
                  three years despite oxygen tank chipped
                        silver
      treasure salvaged from a wreck.

      *

Grief
      too little a word no spring-lock inside it.

Grief
      primed to snap back to its opposite
            the second her eyes open again.

      *

In the next moment
      which he understands at once
            is the beginning of continual afterwards

which is silence arriving
      as Juliet's mother runs out of herself
            and leaves him be

he pulls back the curtain
      and watches the moon shimmy
            over a neat fold in her cloud-sheet.

He sees her decide
        it is time to change her orbit
                and swing closer to Earth.

She whispers to him
        in a white voice like ice hardening on glass
                she has taken over the duties of the sun.

Her bright light will now shine by day
        as well as by night.

And he accepts this
        believing the moon in sympathy
                will rest her entire mass
        against the shell of his chest and be
                weightless.

        *

Injury is the word that occurs first   injury
        then accident
                when he goes to the party after all
                        it is what his father thinks best.

Injury when Juliet's mother
        spins away in a red-flare exhaust-ghost snow-flap
                relieved
                        he understands.

Accident when he passes into a stranger's house
        he thinks might not exist
                except as a stack of crammed and shining rooms
                        bolted together with very loud music.

Although when it comes to the sitting-room dance floor
        edged with a Stonehenge sideboard
            which will never be the same
                after that cigarette-end gouging a ruby
                furrow
        words fail him.

He tries under the space-trip disco-ball spangles
        scattering trashy light.

And again in the profound heat and rock-thrash
        clamping shadows and flesh together.

He must tell everyone
        he has this new distinction
            at the top of his lungs if necessary.

Listen   listen
        his mother is dying   probably
            even as he stands here
                his mother is dying.

But the room   the entire house
        decides this is not important
            and music drowns it.

            *

Juliet will not have it either
        he must be cheerful
            he must be occupied
                he must be   taken out of himself.

So in the run-up to midnight after someone has dimmed
    the lights
        in the maze of a slow song
            she lays her long bare arms on his shoulders
                allowing him to breathe
the sleepy vanilla scent in the crease of her elbows
        linking her fingers behind his neck
            resting her head on his forehead
                her black hair
                    her skin sealed to his skin
            as if her thoughts could flood him
with the perfect blank of superior happiness.

        *

It is embarrassing or
            maybe shameful
        when they slither into the deep cracked back seat
            of her mother's Rover
because at midnight sharp she has come to collect them
            and he discovers after a mile or two
        Juliet is no longer noticeable to him.

Not really
    noticeable.

Not compared to the silence
    as witch trees weave their way home into a tunnel.

Not compared to doubly darkened air
    sharpening pin-prick foxy eyes
        in the fuel gauge and speedometer.

Not compared to Juliet's mother
        sparking a cigarette
                then milling open her window
        and the quick night traces
still outdone by blurry smoke whiff.

Not compared
                now he turns his head and ignores Juliet
                        entirely
        to the lane behind them
                        the underworld mouth
                where rear lights flare gravel under narrowing
                        branches
        and a wreckage wake of his mother's possessions

                her riding jacket   her red collar
                her hairnet   her sheepskin slippers
                her stock   her gold pin with the fox mask
                her black velvet hard hat

her whole wardrobe of everything in fact

not much for a life

vanishes along with the moment he sees it
        the glutinous pasty clay
                that stretches and grabs.

2.

After forty years Juliet emails him
        can they meet.

He reads her message again   and again
            counts.

Forty years
        since their first   last
            lamplight sweating on oak panels
        and the moon intriguing a leaded window.

Four zero
        since her not   slithering black hair
            creamy bare shoulders
                big soft wide not
mouth.

            *

St Pancras station   the Booking Office bar her idea
        where he arrives early like a fool
            giddy a bit
                thanks to the head-back stare
                    at the barrel vault roof
                and sunset's lilacs and charcoals
        staining the many-coloured glass.

Or are they ghosts of the steam age?

At any rate he expects to kill time
        inspecting John Betjeman
                coming or going or both
                        in his flapping bronze mac
                trainspotting the Eurostar
        fly-blown chisel-face of the future.

        *

But Juliet is before him.

It must be Juliet surely
        trailing in one hand her overnight wheelie bag
                the other
                        clamped to a mobile
        husband probably
                in Paris or wherever.

And why not
        except his disappointment exists
                and is frankly
with his tail and whatever else tucked between his legs
        scandalous even to him.

Also why not   Juliet is wearing dark glasses.

Very big   black-framed
        curved
                very dark dark glasses
        masking her face
                as far as possible.

But that is all he has time for.

                    Bye   she says
her first word
        to the phone naturally
                    Bye
as her wheels trundle to a halt
        and he imagines himself replying
                when in fact he is silent
        and staring.

        *

Not her hand
        smuggling the mobile into the slit
                of a navy overcoat pocket.

Not the beautiful black bob
        grey at the roots.

Not the mouth   again not the mouth
        thinned under its lipstick twirl
                think of the millions of breaths
        the words
                smoking over her lips
                        think of feet wearing a threshold.

He is staring at scars on her face.

Scars dicing into her lips
        little hairline fractures
                glaze cracks
                        fissures and faults
                not faults
        scars.

What happened.

These are his first words
        after forty years.

            What happened.

*

Juliet's hair shakes
        blooms in a bridling pony-toss
            then soothes
        and fits neatly again.

Therefore
        he pretends he has seen nothing
            and with a bluff enthusiasm
                which for all she knows
                is now his natural everyday manner
        steers her into the bar of the Booking Office
and round to a
                    bloody miracle
        empty corner table
without another word spoken.

    *

In their background
        departure times and destinations
            deploy watery echoes.

In their immediate vicinity
    high-gloss woodwork   new olde England
       horse-brasses
         and everyone taking a breather.

He follows suit.

He orders house white
    and the waitress who understands speed is the
      essence
        rattles it down
           in a seriously nervous silver ice-bucket.

     *

Grief he remembers
    the strange contentment of living in suffering
      without the possibility
    of such unhappiness
      in whatever remained of life.

Grief even providing
    a peculiar pleasure sometimes
      like the buzz a mind feels
    when a tongue
      slides over a painful tooth.

Grief whispering he might be content
    to live in a mirror-bright shining steel universe
      that could never be altered.

     *

Juliet meanwhile
        eases her dark glasses
            a fraction along her nose
                and rests them on a pale skin-ridge
            the main scar there
    to hide it.

She has no time to waste
        and without the least flourish or sidestep
            delivers a boiled-down recitative
        namely   her life since last they met
            and parted.

        Au pair   marriage
        two children   girls
        living in   freelance
        films   documentaries mostly.

    *

He shuffles his glass on the table top
            creased apparently
        with ghostly cloth wipes
and cannot prevent himself
        still looking
            when he thinks she is not looking.

Hair sweetly hooked behind one ear.

Jittery ear stud on its plump little flesh cushion.

White throat   very white throat
        swelling when she swallows
                in the shadowy collar V
                        of her expensive black silk shirt.

Surprising   forgotten
        blunt-tipped   almost square-ended fingers
        nails painted   milky suns
                rising from the cuticle.

        *

Then it is his turn he thinks
        but that is not what she came for.

She stalls him.

She slips off her dark glasses
                and shows him her white face
                        naked.

        *

If she told him a wildcat
        launching out of a pine forest

if she told him a lightning strike
        a firework
                an alleyway bottle-lunge

if she told him a particularly sharp idea
        an idea like a star bursting
                the most brilliant idea imaginable
had shattered out of her brain
                through her left cheek
        engulfed her left eye
and scorched her mouth

he would believe her.

But   a company car
        the M40 late at night
                darkness   rain
        and roly-poly down the embankment
                outside High Wycombe

High
        Wycombe

which Juliet offers
        without him asking
                he cannot accept
and must.

        *

No sooner
        the wet tarmac rubber smear
                the barrier can-opened
                        the mud gouge   the grass rip
        the steaming hush and electrical dashboard glow
than his mother again
        in the seamless flash footage
                he cannot avoid quoting by heart.

Head shaved gingery bare
    tiger-slash operation scar
        eyes pulpy   bruise-mashed
  oxygen   tank   tube   mask
        oxygen itself
pressing a skeletal finger to pursed lips

      sssssssssssshhhhhhhh.

    *

Which Juliet has no time for
      insisting the point is not
        only her accident   the point is
    after that she lay unconscious three days.

Midwinter fields   no footprint
      among flint bones
        and bristly Essex clay lumps
  no shadow
  only the seething snow surface
      opening
    and closing its lacy arms.

Unconscious Juliet continues
    then awake but not
      awake-awake   not
        herself.

More like a radio dial twiddling
	picking on day one
		a French signal
	and her voice speaking French only
on day two
	her voice in English
		with a French accent

on day three normal
	her everyday voice
		beaming back to her
			from the spangling gas-warps
	of infinite deep brain space.

	*

A waitress at the table adjacent
	clears cutlery like glittery fish in a handful.

He meanwhile
	sponges up what he hears.

He wrings out Juliet's language
	and squeezes it into his own language
		storing it
			along with the car wreck
	the rain the rain the rain the headlights
		stubbed in embankment plough.

Although
    as the debris
        the confetti windscreen glass
            the smashed boxer's face fender
                the car radio
        churning its excitable jabber regardless
           and   in the midst of it all
Juliet's silence
        her scarred face   her unconsciousness

    as the combined tangle of this groans
        creaks
        scrapes
        sinks
        settles
        and enters his consciousness

he reminds himself
        Juliet is not his punishment.

Not if he chooses.

    *

At which point
    she arrives at the point
        that brought her here in the first place.

She tells him   at last and suddenly
    she can remember nothing
        of her life before the accident.

She explains
        having forgotten everything herself
            her sister remembered
                she knew him once.

She asks him what passed   please
            between them

she is in his hands
            she says.

        *

Whereupon he straightens to meet Juliet's eye
        meaning
            he enters her eye and drops
                down through liquid green-flecked chestnut brown
                    into the dead centre.

Which is prepared to believe him
        albeit a cat look
            I know you   do I know you
                remind me.

And he deliberates.
        weighing her featherweight weight.

He deliberates
        then lets her go.

He lets her life go
        and Juliet in their time remaining
                bare-faced   dressed in her wounds
                    leans forward
to catch what he has to say.

2.

Waders

In days that follow, when the summer brings
slow afternoons with nothing left to do,
I take what used to be your garden chair
and park it underneath the wayward ash
tipped forward where the garden swerves
to hide the house from view. In secret then
I conjure up the notebook I have found
among your bedside things and open it.
Blank pages. Thoughts you never had. Or had
but could not bring yourself to say. Should I
imagine them or write my own instead?
I close my eyes and scrutinise the white
that also lies inside me while the ash
rattles its pale green keys above my head.

*

The milk float with its thin mosquito whine
straining through larch and elder from the lane,
the anxious bottles in their metal basket
intent on music but without a tune,
the milkman in his doctor's grubby coat
and sailor's rakish dark blue canvas cap,
are all invisible, imagined/dreamed
beyond my curtains in the early light,
along with tissue footprints in the frost,
our rinsed-out empties, and the rolled-up note
exchanged for bottles with their silver tops
the blue tits have already broken through
to sip the stiffened plugs of cream before
we come downstairs and bring our order in.

*

To think the world is endless, prodigal,
to part the hedgerow-leaves and see the eggs
like planets in a crowded galaxy,
to hear my mother's voice advising me
the mother-bird herself will never mind
if I take only one and leave the rest,
means nothing more than showing interest.
As does the careful slow walk home, the ritual
of pinpricks through both ends, the steady breath
that blows the yolk and albumen clean out
but keeps the pretty shell intact, the nest
of crumpled paper in the cedar drawer,
the darkness falling then, the hush, and me
bringing the weight of my warm mind to bear.

*

Before our time they used my room to store
apples collected from those crooked trees
now wading waist deep at the garden end
in frilly white-capped waves of cow parsley,
and laid them out in rows not touching quite.
I guess all this because the floorboards show
wherever they had missed one as it turned
to mush that sank a stain into the wood.
My bed stands over them and when at night
my eyes grow used to darkness they appear:
the Coxes, Bramleys, Blenheim Oranges
whose names alone can fill the empty air
with branches weighted down by next year's crop
that turn its scent half-cloying and half-sweet.

*

I try my father's waders on for size
then take, with him encouraging, his rod
and wading stick, his canvas bag, his cap
rigid beneath its crown of favourite flies,
and step into the river. From the bank
he says I look like him. As for myself
I only think of how to stand upright
with water hardening one second round
my ankles, and the next uprooting me
as though I have no purchase on the world.
My father shouts, Don't fight it. I obey.
I let the deluge settle round my heart
then lay me on my back to carry me
round the long sweep beyond my father's sight.

*

That roofless kennel where the nettles shake
their fine-haired leaves and tiny tight green buds.
That almost-buried path of blood-red bricks
where ivy scrawls across its own designs.
That ruined square of cracked disrupted blocks
where once a summer house turned round and stared.
These were the former glories of the house
although I like their fall and brokenness
much more than grieving for a time I missed.
As also I like walking with the ghosts
that wander through the garden everywhere –
the mother and her son whose footsteps leave
no prints beside us in the grass as though
our selves are all the company we keep.

On Her Blindness

Too faint for you the face-print on the glass
left by the owl that thought your kitchen light
was moonshine and would surely let him pass
in one piece through the house from night to night.

The Ring

Soon my father will lose his wedding ring
but before that happens we take the path
along the cliff-edge past the sign that says
Danger: Keep Back because the waves below
have undermined it, and the next big storm
will be enough to bring the whole face down.

I know this but I can't help looking down
and noticing how each wave throws a ring
of primrose foam that's nothing like a storm
round fallen rocks forming a sort of path
for someone who might find themselves below –
which no one ever would, my father says.

It's much too dangerous, my father says,
new rock-falls any time might tumble down
and injure them, and while the sea below
looks calm, a quickly rising tide would ring
and terrify them, devastate their path,
then drown them just as surely as a storm.

I hear him out about the calm and storm
and fall in line with everything he says,
continuing along the cliff-top path
until it leads us in a zigzag down
onto the seashore where a wormy ring
of sand recalls the tunnelling below.

My father says the North Sea is below
freezing almost, thanks to a recent storm,
and so he eases off his wedding ring
because the cold is bound to shrink, he says,
his fingers, and his ring would then slip down
and vanish like the dangerous cliff path.

He turns around to see once more the path,
the dizzy fall, the rocks, the waves below.
He thinks his only choice is to set down
on one stone of the many that the storm
has carried from the North Sea bed, which says
a lot about the power of storms, his ring.

It slides down out of sight as though the storm
has also switched his path to run below.
This neither of us says. He never finds his ring.

Chincoteague

Walking in Chincoteague among the reeds
stitching thin air and sunlight into shade
I thought of Tabitha the seamstress dead,
Saint Peter at her bedside calling out
Get up! – which led me suddenly to you
on winter evenings from the time before,
hunched in a cone of yellow light, one hand
poising your needle like a trophy saved
from chaos that might any moment now
descend again, the other with a thread
you lifted to your pouting lips and kissed
to dampen and make sharp enough to pierce
the needle's eye before you pulled it tight,
and took a breath, and cut the thread in two.

In the Family

Like accelerated Proust
(just scenes, no thinking),
or like too-fast drinking,
my old mind lays waste

habits of logical progression,
and instead accidentally slips
or decides to leap
from now-Andrew-Motion

into a previous I
via the apparently ample supply
of scenes reminding me
that I saw you die

even during those pretty times
when death
might either have been saving breath
or losing its true aim.

That day in the greenhouse, e.g.,
when I stepped up close
to discover how you chose
in the seedling tray

which young green shoots
to keep and encourage
and which sickly ones to scotch,
but also felt the weight

during that sensitive decision
of your bare thumb
turning further and further down
with tremendous precision

into the dark earth,
which then duly swallowed
the tail of frail white roots
before the rest of you followed.

2.

Only this morning
we scuffled again:
my brother, myself,
on Mersea Island,

crouched in the lee
of a derelict pillbox,
that line of defence
deflecting the wind.

The North Sea fumed
in its ravenous bed;
decoy gulls
hung stiff in the wind.

But nothing stopped
the moment of truth,
and to beat the cold
my brother adopted

a thick tweed cap.
Top of the morning
he mouthed to waves
which included me,

then hoisted his cap
before fitting it back
with his face aghast
and starting for France.

3.

At the bend of the stairs
I turned my gaze
to the gravel outside,
where a red-faced man

stood with the fruit
he had stopped to steal
from our apple tree,
then back to the fly

on the windowpane
I had just this minute
squashed with my thumb
and discovered its guts

had the same dull grey
as the coils that oozed
from a firework I liked
called Vesuvius,

while my father agreed
in the kitchen below –
ignoring the fact
I might overhear –

with my mother cooking
he thought that now
I had reached the age
worth listening to.

The Bee Tree

American linden alias American lime,
the family basswood, *tilia americana,*
a handsome and deciduous street tree

with rugged bark in elephantine ridges
and russet twigs adopting green until,
when flowering, it amplifies with bees

that, as they tune their soporific song
and load their golden panniers, reveal
the tree knew what its name was all along.

*

Breezy with insouciant twitches
the example below my room
is playing the part of Summer,
flouncing her new feather boa

catching the eye of her paramour,
me, glued in the frame of my window
to see if a rival appears and is caught
in the black silk net of her shadow.

*

Loving a thing
I know is when
a becomes the.

The tree in view
I know is what
I love to see.

    *

One night and then for a week after
a young grey heron with no idea
of the right and wrong place to live
takes up residence in the branches.

Only occasional passers-by below
pay any attention; mostly they see
a heavy white shit-trail and assume
it was sparrows making a bivouac.

Eventually I will realise my duty here
is to understand reality as it appears,
and see the puzzle is not what goes
where. The problem is one of scale.

    *

In one account
the gods of Earth
cascaded down
on silken threads

and came to rest
in leaves of trees.
I witnessed them
in what became

a final blaze
of sun today –
a razor sheen,
here, then gone.

I want no more.
The life of things
will never speak
in any tongue.

*

Wearing a bright orange hi-vis jacket,
the leaf-blower dismisses fallen leaves
from left to right along the sidewalk,

while the wind with no colour or form
orders them back in the other direction
to settle beneath the tree once more.

*

First thing and last thing
at this time of year
a skein of Canada geese fly
over my roof and the tree

squeezing their rubber horns.
It is what I expect to hear
but the tree looks up amazed,
her dark fountain frozen.

So much extravagant move-
ment and all of it chosen!
In the aftermath a breeze
kicks off a different scene,

but the most branches do
is to stir very sluggishly,
as spars of flotsam will
in the weak hands of the sea.

*

This late in autumn
she wears a contraption
made of gold leaf,
but even such glamour
is never enough
to keep her from harm.

The faintest breath
of dishevelling air
and she's poor again,
a shivering waif
whose one ambition
remains to be warm.

*

As the tree points her bare arms
like a sinner appealing
to heaven

she makes her final count:
four pumpkin-brown leaves
and a fifth distressed green.

Beauty now depends on relation,
with her head unbowed
and these rags her crown.

*

Like my love when she takes off her ring
and lays it on the nightstand beside our bed,
the tree places her last leaf on the sidewalk
and stands completely naked wanting to play.

*

In one interruption
a buzz-saw echoes
from Domino Sugars
across the harbour:

maybe the sound
of a sugar tree sliced
into saleable logs –
that mechanical whizz

and saccharine crash.
But this is a thought
I keep to myself
and the tree never has.

*

When winter ends
I plunge my hand
inside the tree
and neighbours think
I'm about to snatch
a dove from a hat.

It's not like that.
I'm testing heat
and degrees of dark
to see if they match
the kind of box
I have in mind.

                *

How are you today
is the question arising
from the street below
but only today carries.

How am I today,
which is not yesterday,
and still less tomorrow,
although not separate.

I wish it were otherwise.
I wish I could snap free
from the long link-chain
of time's old fuckery.

To live without guilt,
sure, but also to quench
hope with its curled tongue
slavering to become.

Give me the green tree
again. Give me the word
now rising through shade
that finishes in sun.

3.

Randomly Moving Particles

That Christmas I ran through fire in London,
carrying my old father across my shoulders.
My mother too, she followed. You alive alas,
I could not bring.

*

Flight attendants wear Santa hats, Rudolph ears,
and keep straight faces during the emergency drills.
In the easy weeping that arrives with high altitude
grief is not too powerful a word. I grieve for you
in the life left behind, the existence diminishing.

I hear the cirrus I fly through crackle like dry clay
and planets squealing on their pivots in deep space.

I set my watch five hours behind. Eventually I sleep.

*

The Maryland coast below my plane losing height,
pleasure boats in the miniature expensive harbours
baring white teeth in green mouths dropped open,

then suburbs working avenues into close-knit tweed,
leaves all fallen, blue swimming pools glaring empty,
is changing to was, bluntly reformed parts of speech,

nouns being ocean now, adjectives wide, and emails
stacked in thin air waiting for my phone to wake up
as the facts of my life are occluded within my life.

     *

There is no river flowing. There is infinite block time
and a decisive spotlight-finger pointing now to this
minute now to another.

                                Also there is jet lag,
a clothes-bag of soft grey linen filled with hammers
dragged by their own weight down the marble brain.

     *

Baltimore Department of Transportation what the fuck.

Odd potholes maybe but entire gravel trenches
really.

Jiggly loose brick crossings, dolphin-backed
   tarmac humps,
scoops, cobble runs, bare mud even
really.

Then downtown past the haunted high rises and
   blind eyes
of Gotham-Golgotha scattering underground
   steam-bursts,
last gasps exhaling whatever Ratking is snacking
   on beneath,

concrete and fenders, gravel titbits, knocked-off exhausts,

until finally out and through into widening
    brighter light
I go with gorgeous silvery Chesapeake sky
    overreaching.

                *

Snow begins, throwing down blank pages
to make clear the wind's advances,
paw-prints and strangers, never you close.

The second day in my life I shall not live
through entirely, the hours less than 24,
is beginning when. I would like to be told.

My shadow has severed its ties and taken off
over the whiteness arriving. I am not afraid.
A point continues when it has no other part.

                *

Four billion miles from the sun
making it the most remote planetary flypast in history
New Horizons has surveyed Ultima Thule
from a distance of 2,200 miles.

Its shape is a contact binary
which is to say two touching bodies.

It is a russet colour
caused by the exposure of hydro-molecules
to sunlight over millions of years.

Originally an agglomeration of pebbles
it coalesced into successively larger bodies
until only two remained.

These gradually travelled towards each other
and merged in a walking speed kiss
more like docking than collision.

*

When my sleep begins I return to the front gate
watching you fold down into your car and drive off.
Breath-mist on the windows. A phantom of exhaust.
A liquid trail I could have used to track you.

Instead I take myself inside and lean on the door-back
in the new and weirdly high definition of time in solitary.

The pathos of a dumped umbrella still sparky with rain.

Grey daylight in the bedroom becoming a block of ice
trimmed and polished to the same precise dimensions.

With so much malice in natural law, I had half-expected to turn
to the Atlantic sky passing and see you miles below me
like a drowned woman in a well, endlessly the same,
endlessly falling.

*   *   *

Punctual as the evening star
a Baltimore Police helicopter
fingers the surface of the harbour.

In long dark before spring arrives,
a skinned log, chewed off and leprous,
offers itself as a ray of sunlight trapped.

*

Here is the old question of leave or remain,
which way madness lies, which way I lose
what exactly I cannot decide, years for a starter,
also skin flakes, hair certainly, accumulated wisdom,
everything gathered by my own efforts, everything
stripped from me in the fall here, in the rise here,
except this hard nub of myself, this clay moulded
by first contact with life I have now turned away.

*

My father himself in his last hours,

soft-spoken always and that rarely

but lucid and definite when he does,

why has it come to this why this,

and me in silence returning his echo.

*

In the small hours I turn back to face the mirror
and see again the pictures I have taken of our time
with my mind's eye flicker across its silver screen.
Someone outside is using an electric saw to chop
a pipe in two at this implausibly late hour. I hear
the piece he wants strike the road and echoes fly.

Then a couple arguing run past but he is too fast
and catches her, although she loudly fights him off
and manages to escape. When I pull up the blind
that has concealed me from the man inspecting flats
opposite, I see above the expanding ripple of roofs
the moon gathering its fragments, fling them away.

*

Now snow has melted and frost retreats
piecemeal down my street to the harbour
where wind is blustering the water black,
ancient water rising beneath new water,
shouldering it aside slippery and slight,
asserting what is deep down and inviting,
whispering in the old defeated languages,
remembering the islands made of oysters,
cod shoals packed in tight and the pilgrims
walking dryshod ashore on heads and tails.

*

The Japanese spacecraft Hayabusa2, having
    spiralled down
and landed on the asteroid Ryugu, has fired successfully
a tantalum bullet weighing 0.2 ounces into the
    rock's surface
and collected the debris using its specialised
    sampling horn.

The goal is to better understand the solar system's history
and evolution, the role that carbon-rich asteroids played
in the emergence of life on Earth, and to pioneer methods
of harvesting valuable minerals and metals for future use.

*

I come to the pool in the quiet hour after 2 p.m.
when the lanes are empty and the surface still,
except where clean water, piped from below,
produces pressure like veins figuring marble,
invisible within but creaturely as skinship itself.

You are absent here too, your fingerprints sanded,
no further evidence available, the very idea of you
a cork pushed down in a wine bottle, a dark secret,
a precious life tilted and sliding, tilted and sliding.

*

The President's team has enlarged his hands
by screwing with photos then released online.
Meanwhile the man himself in the Rose Garden
wears his mobster's overcoat and wide red tie
knotted so the tongue falls long and slendering.
Optics! Optics! But my sight endlessly running,
my eye divided in bad home reception, finds also
the PM scurrying to frame an opposite idea, power
swelling in diminishment. Optics, dammit, optics!

* * *

Snowdrops among other things in waist-high civic beds.

A gaggle of novices pleading for the remission of sins.

A congregation of angels who sing in the spring wind
canticles no one can hear.

Otherwise sneaks of light
escaped from the underworld, the flickering glimpse
dying in life allows.

*

What language is spoken in this place? It seems close
to mine but I can seldom be heard, and when heard
am never well understood. People laugh uproariously
then wobble off with their busy hams jostling together.
Veterans accost me. I meet a sad clown by the harbour
strumming an electric guitar, and his amplified music
troubles the wheels of the universe like loose gravel.

*

The Chinese rover and lander
have taken pictures of each other
on the dark far side of the moon.

The Chinese say their spacecraft
is in good working order
and the rover has just woken
from a period on standby.

Images make the landscape appear reddish,
a far cry from gunpowder,
the detectors are less sensitive to blue and green.

Thanks to tidal locking
we see only one face of the moon from Earth
meaning among other things the moon
takes exactly as long to rotate on its axis
as it does to complete an orbit of the Earth.

The far side is much more rugged than the near
with a thicker and older crust
more widely pocked with craters.

*

I take to Gunpowder River in the early season,
following a rail-trail navvies bullied clean through,
boulders of their blasts encumbering the stream,
bud-casings stippling the quick mahogany flummox,
trout sunk deep down, stunned by the priestly cold,
then step into the same element myself regardless.

There is the impression of sousing, of compressing,
and the valley widens from dead centre, the idea
of you opening also, my line signing up to blank air
before quizzing among stones and tricky stick-jams,
looping wherever the current loops, extricating,
then enquiring again, the trout starved no doubt
but making do, something else I have to tell you.

*

There is the world behind
with its water-bug dimple
and airy scuttle.

There is the world to come
where home remains to be seen.

There are days passing
and days when the clock sticks.

There are the small mercies
of WhatsApp and FaceTime
and the kindness of children.

There is the friendly arrow-shower daily
of email somewhere becoming correspondence
that ascends to survive in the iCloud.

There is nowhere. There is never.

*

My father on his deathbed.

My father when his body-machinery is working
just,
but his mind
he abandoned,
while preparing to set his jaw
and turn his face to the wall.
Hospice wall that is,
cherry blossom pink
thanks to the one ebullient tree
crashing the windowpane.
My father who fought and bravely once upon a time.

My father who carried his myriad astounding griefs
and never says a word.

        *

More than 40% of the planet's insects are now in decline
at a rate 8 times faster than mammals, birds and reptiles,
amounting to a collapse of 2.5% every year for the last 30.

This biomass presently outweighs humanity by 17 times
and includes bees, butterflies, caddisflies, dragonflies,
        stoneflies,
flies and beetles – of which there are 350,000 different
        varieties.

There are always some species that take advantage of
        a vacuum
left by other species, but all the evidence points in
        one direction.
In 10 years a quarter of what we have; in 50 half;
        in 100 none.

＊

The cigarette slip-stream, acrid but desirable,
of some bastard blocking the sidewalk ahead.
Sun blinding my eyes like a rage of hot metal.
Poor service and cherry tomatoes spongy
in Whole Foods well before their sell-by date.
Crap music in the pool annihilating thought.
You not here. Your taste under my fingernail
tentative but definite as yellow cowslip scent.

＊   ＊   ＊

I tell myself be more adventurous and march north,
south, east and west (east is the harbour so a dead end)
but soon balk at the limits of my safety, which I know
by smoke signals that arise from smouldering tyres.

I revert to my old new ways and find comfort in that
but the question keeps arriving: What am I doing here.
I often repeat myself and the answer still escapes me.

＊

The Eastern Seaboard drowned in line with the I-95,
hothouse existence, sketchy burials, rocket plumes,
then gravity drag and a dependable tablet for sleep,
narrowing eyes losing sight of the bluest eye closed,
and the cloud-cover prompt with its kindly veils.

The planet FarFarOut, 140 times further from the sun,
10 times the mass of Earth, the furthest object known
in the solar system, the boundary of our power to see,
much mooted, previously known simply as Planet Nine,
definite but sheltering in the Oort cloud, very faint.

*

Here I am always and continuously beginning.

Here I am dressed in a skimpy little garment
made of what ideas and work I do this instant.

Here I am looking beyond the pale of my existence
at the undefended life to come I can only imagine.

Here I am repetitive while seriously bewildered.

Here I am corrupt yet become unearthly innocent.

*

I sweep back again
up the tarmac path between headstones
to my father's grave and mother's beside.

My father however
still wearing the Irish tweed suit
with surprisingly loud orange stripes
and regimental tie in which he was buried
is busy.

He has chosen this exact moment
to burrow through the rotten wall of my mother's grave
and raise her in his arms again.

Or quite possibly he repeats this action
every minute of every day.

In either case it is a delicate operation
and requires his complete concentration.

My mother after all
is kicked-in and crushed along the left side of her head
a glittering pulp,
a ruination,
and everything she stores there
is leaking out through her ear
which she would very much like to stop
at all costs. For which reason

my father turns to me and says
he is sorry
but now it is simply too late
to give his attention to anything else.

                *

Where have you been, your particles whizzing off
     everywhere,
touching some delicately, brushing others. I know
     your ways,
I have tracked your zigzags and circuits, my skin
     remembering,
a butterfly woken from its cranny by delirious spring
     sunlight
now clasped on the window sipping its black pool
     of shadow.

                *

O Trump is he still here, this time dry-humping the flag,
goofily beaming, lavishing his love, false, chuntering on,

the flow remarkably free of impediment, almost devoid
of dead air, of -um and -ah and -er, unctuous, dictatorial,
abandoning threads mid-phrase, returning or maybe not,
having the fluency of relatively unmonitored spontaneity,

false, lacking the normal signs of difficulty in
    thinking what
to say when performing the chosen word-stream,
    less talk-
talk than sing-song, abandoning phrases and starting
    points,

spasmodic, self-interrupting, false, severely unintelligible
as explicit statement but highly expressive by implication,

false, egocentric and inconsiderate, never showing teeth
when smiling, smiling seldom, lifting corners of the mouth.

        *

I climb onto my roof to count the stars
and see beyond them the gas nebulae
flaring like ideas that start before words
and instantly die.

Then I wake up and become Elpenor
for the twinkling of an eye.

It is past midday and the ship has gone.
Come back I shout but there is no one.

So I climb back down to the ground
but miss my step on the ladder
and break my neck.

Now who will lay me out to rest
in my beautiful armour.

Now who will keep me from dreaming
lives that can never be mine.

These are the questions I put to the sand
as it pours through the bones of my hand.

Questions I put to the shade
of the oar that grows in the earth above my head.

* * *

Because I carried my father from the flames.
Because I am dredging memory and glad to.
Because I respond to the gravitational pull
(chewing my fingernails admittedly, asking
have I eaten my own body-weight). Because
my mother followed. Because I live dead days.

*

As surprising really but in its way as simple
as a god moving among his earthly inferiors,
a flock of sparrows bursts from a dust-bowl
and sinks into bare branches of a sycamore.
Dark matter of randomly moving particles.
A god whose elements, ashen in silhouette,
produce a scratchy melody that decorates

my time in passing, if not the proof a god
has left his engine running while he vanishes
to look for something elsewhere he forgot.

*

Ripley, an anthropomorphic test device, rides again
aboard the SpaceX Dragon, fitted out with sensors
around the head, neck and spine to record everything
an astronaut would experience during the mission.
Look forward to meeting you, tweets Anne McClain
from the International Space Station. My mouth
meanwhile, recalling vertebrae of your turned back,
becomes my own by dark degrees, soured, lived in,
but daylight cannot be helped now, the Earth ignites,
and the SpaceX Dragon's soft capture gets under way,
docking with a spring system that dampens movement,
then deploying clever hooks to create an air-tight seal.

*

Computer says no and that gets a laugh
so parliament tries it. When parliament
says no the world splits its sides. Then
parliament says no to no and melancholy
seeps from the centre out like the black
stain in the eye of a pansy flower. Blame
what. Wars and that. Silver sea bollocks.
Blame the national psychic head-wound
bleeding for generations until the brain,
starved of oxygen, intentionally dreams
only of green mountains, arrows and bows
burnished, the word yes no longer assayed.

On FaceTime in your white jumper and black
silk shirt with the lacy neck akin to a nightie.
No one can tell the temperature of a blue sky
simply by looking. A restored film of soldiers
fighting in 1914–18 shows their terrible teeth.
A child has chickenpox. The question of leave
or remain has become a free vote. Every single
soldier in that ditch beneath the flowering may
has 30 minutes to live. We are more sensitive
to noise now than when we were young. I have
lost you. You have lost me. No, I am here again.

*

At the end of the harbour
sunset has caught fire,
and ladders on light hinges
drop from sky attics.

But angels fluff their ascent
and the god loses patience,
stamping through his floor
to ensure evening deepens.

*

Beyond the ring-road a dinosaur fly-past,
a gull finding a thermal to wander the city,
and across the further distance a freight train
sings America's grace note and defining music.
I am homesick for the future. I have torn up
the foundations of my life and stand on them

now scouring the wall of the horizon, or now
staring into the bare tree outside my window
where dead branches in the crown gesticulate
with stiff arthritic jabs while others living sway.
It is midday meanwhile and weak sunlight slaps
down into the harbour but mostly reflects back
into the sky greasy but simplified. The bars open
and first customers arrive. A cormorant passes.

*

But a story with no story, how can that end well?
If a diary there is death, if correspondence death,
the moon wearing thin in her threadbare shawl.

The bright instantiation of things incomplete,
of life that remains unlived, the end in sight.
Less and less the conviction of rounding out.

More and more the sense of a widening sky.
Rotation and fixity. Bafflement. Fear. The moon
returning to show again the face I saw just now.

*

I lie in the prow and look down. Water
at this point in the harbour is so clear
I can easily imagine my fingers reaching
to touch the gravel bed that lies below.

This is the rim of the Earth before the fall.
My bow-wave swells each and every pebble,
where timid creatures sensing my approach
burrow and wait for the threat I am to go.

4.

Evening Traffic

He stopped dead in heavy evening traffic,
leaving his truck unlocked at the roadside
and weaving his way between raindrops
into the cavernous bed store adjacent.

I thought before the lights changed
he looked in that instance like a man
from ancient history frozen in a glacier,
but then I only glanced up for a moment.

In truth he was trying out a new mattress,
seizing the chance to stretch flat on his back
with both hands clasped behind his head
and drumming his heels if I'm not mistaken.

    *

I continued to the end of South Ann,
then pulled over by the harbour wall
near the building site of the new hotel.

A US Navy destroyer had tied up there,
a sleek beast with both its gun turrets
shrouded in sheets of grey mackintosh.

There was no sign of any crew on deck
but I swear I smelled cigarette smoke,
just a delicate thread or two lingering.

I suppose they must have passed my way,
passed through the girls waiting I mean,
and been invited by them, and continued.

*

I lay down later on my own bed to sleep,
but ever since the autumn cold arrived
and those hefty leaves fell from the vine
that sprawls in summer along my fence,

an extremely bright light that shines
all night above the parking lot opposite
and the empty cars glittering like waves
also sends its blaze across my ceiling.

What the hell. I put on my eye-shade
as if composing myself for a night flight
and drop down fast beneath the harbour
to stay there among its darkling rocks.

When I look upwards I see schools of fish
in one mind while they change direction,
and sunlight in a dimpled ring as if hands
were washing there, or reaching through.

The Catch

Tangier Island, Chesapeake Bay

Set out early
harbour dock slop
then waves full whack
through painter holes.

West Ridge to port
Uppards to starboard
that stand of pines
clean knocked down.

Valuable uprights
along with grave-stones
bones return there
rolled in surf.

Violet marshes
courtship nests
a baseball diamond
ghostly drowned.

*

Who saw this spray
as a willow branch
its feathery swag
more seeding grass.

Who lived from the start
among arrowheads
worshipped in old ways
lay with tornadoes.

Now precious little
and language a sandpiper
peep peep peep
prints last no time.

*

Ravenous waves
run for deep water
fibreglass booming
reliable enough.

But think of death
sometimes desire it
flat earth edges
withering away.

Flow becoming
everything becoming
not a blade left
not a grain of sand.

Still gorse in bloom
last of its kind
and wind hissing through
annihilation.

*

Open the brain lid
glimpse the idea
big sky and waves
flicker like snow.

A long way home
with the island gone
sea hawks free
to fish dead centre.

This hull meanwhile
crazy with sand grains
worked-in hairs
serving its purpose.

All aboard crab-catch
burned match eyes
blue arms poised
definitely feisty.

*

But think of home
love-cry ascending
touch still dragging
heart by the root.

Envisage the world
as wind across water
where galaxies swim
in the plainest surface.

*

Spray beads shake
their dots of sky
all fall down
damned to pieces.

White roofs now
sleek as leaves
a flood extending
the hungry stream.

Face in the window
that feathery too
the eye delighting
a lifetime longer.

The mind still sounding
one green hill
though belonging knows
what follows after.

The White Bear

When I discovered his tracks in the ice-field
        they appeared to have no beginning
and ended in pure black water.

Without hesitation I knelt down
        and stared into the trembling deep.

I saw him swim through darkness
      with immense and steady strokes
        the violence of his body
redeemed by phosphorescence
        glowing throughout his pelt

by a slipstream of sand
        and small particles of rock
      such as also appear in the night sky
        when meteors are scudding overhead.

    *

One day
        in the course of his earthly existence
        he lived in solitude eating snow

the next
        he was accompanied by replicas of himself
        grazing the tundra like hogs on a common

one day
> he held his breath underwater for hours
> striking his prey from below like a waterspout

the next
> he had fooled them into thinking his nose
> was the black dot of a seal dozing on the
> horizon

one day
> he shunted before him ice-blocks the size of cars
> and used them as a shield that made him
> invisible

the next
> he lifted and hurled these same blocks as
> easily as dice
> and so crushed his victims or battered out
> their brains.

*

In the centuries of worship I meant to represent him
> but only managed to carve my own skeleton.

I touched him in my mind and prized this connection
> but realised my fear was his greatest gift to me.

I regularly ingested a part of his body with all due
ceremony
> but suffered abysmal headaches and lost patches
> of my skin.

*

For these reasons among others
        I have chosen not to prevent him
            escaping from me entirely.

I have closed my ears and eyes
        when the ice-floes groan
            and glaciers express their gigantic grief.

When the earth stalls and grinds on its axis
        and vaporous purple lights
            stream from its parching gears.

I have decided to make a new home for myself
            with hot showers and a table
reliable internet connection
        a wardrobe
            and a lifetime of dry clothes.

Among the Others

1.

Starlings
      if not God's finger
    dragged through the skin of the world.

God's breath and flag.

The smoke from God's skidding wheels
    in droops
                and puffs
      and plumes.

Starlings if not
        the sweat of air
    as it wrestles to stop God
      breaking through.

2.

Sparking up in their wisteria sleeping quarters
    fireflies are no match
        for the enormous night falling.

Think of them instead as a treasure hoard
    walled up centuries ago
        and now reflecting something of the lamp
a thief has hoisted in astonishment.

3.

When the meteor struck
            this cormorant skimmed away unscathed
                    hugging the ocean surface
        then dozing on a rock for thirty million years.

Or he dived
        and dried in a pose of crucifixion.

Human questions will die down soon enough.

In the permanent frost of his brain
        that has always been perfectly clear.

Meanwhile
        no singing.

What the Grass Says

I have been talking to you
        a long while now
                but only recently have you begun
                        to pay me serious attention.

It is time
        given that I have grown
                tall enough to peer over
        the wall you built around me.

Every morning and night
        I easily catch your eye
                as you fume past
        in your tedious traffic stream.

I hear
        exactly what you are thinking
although you find it hard
                to admit it to yourself.

I see
        your glance flicker between the headstones
                I carefully attend here
                        with their fading names
                                and unhappy angels.

I know
        you ask yourself what
                would it mean to go to ground
                        in this particular foreign field.

So let me reassure you.

In stillness I am always
                    a reliable green silence
        scarred with minuscule bug-shifts and bird-scratches.

When the wind blows I am ready
                with my repertoire of tongues
                    a sugar spill
                            for a gentle puff
                    seething spits
        for the storm dog and his thunder.

Also
                            I am a humble servant.

Encountering your children in due course
        I promise to flatten under their tread
                    and lie down
        as I would on their natural side of the world.

Also
        I have remarkable ways to please you.

I become silver
                    if the angles are right.

I become gold
                    and violet
                    and lavender.

And if I coarsen in winter
        reduced to a brown mess
                it only goes to show
                    I too have my weakness.

Sometimes I turn myself into a glittering sword
                    at others a feather
                    a bristle
                    a head of hair
                    the claws of a paw.

Sometimes I raise my offspring
                    to resemble the knob of a
                    small stick
        elsewhere I am a wand
                    a midget finger
                    a tickle
                            soft as mouse fur.
Even without trying
        my millions of needling shadows
                weave an enormous dark
        of no particular shape.

If you see me retire like this
        through the debris of myself
                be certain I will revive
                        and bask for ever
        in the bliss of infinite patience.

Hardly a Day

'Despair of Life, the Means of living shows': Virgil,
The Aeneid, *Book 2, line 476, translated by John Dryden*

1.

All time indeterminate now
so this might be late or early
and hardly a day in itself.

Call it infernal nevertheless
with my first move a descent
into air thick with lamentation.

I mean tension in the clock
as it works towards sunrise
and fear becomes natural law.

  *

Sparrows in the tree opposite
are ghosts from hollow graves
where green leaves denote death.

Dawn chorus also a madhouse,
given this scandalous deep hush
and human replies anonymous.

Forget even courtesies of touch
its delicious extended sentence
and bracing diamond textures.

*

Which reminds me to make clear
after speaking droplets of spittle
will stay airborne eight seconds.

Long enough anyone might think
to question what does and does not
remain subject to our attention.

If I mention my old man's hands
with their liver spots and arthritis
is that worth the risk of expression.

*

Interest does inflate a little
in the novelty of insults inflicted
e.g. cuticles cracked with washing,

or specs fogged with breath
funnelled behind the face mask
and if oniony never that good.

Not to mention regions destitute
where the homicide rate holds up
that being too important to fail.

*

There is still noticing however.
There is the shining eye-machine
in the stalled remnants of life.

Impatient I might be elsewhere
but still favour neglected things
and continue democratic in that

littleness being one form of life
on the bleak shore. Or otherwise
inclined to seek the silent floods.

2.

Midday purgatorial stroll allowed
and today's high tide a black cut-out
the harbour at this time exactly fills.

Matching forms and the cormorant
also adaptive in its timely practice
vanishing then bobbing up well fed.

An angel too it goes without saying
there is one skims the glassy wastes
inviting me on shores unknown to lie.

*

Which leaves things where exactly.
Not with a real heaven-sandal
trampling the water mouth,

more likely a lavender yoga nut
head-standing by the dry dock
her world knowingly upside down.

While current in the deep down
never knows what odd beauty
or obstacle might strike it next.

*

The port of entry long since gone
hands pressing for free passage
reefed sails and wonderful land.

Now it is wind over the harbour
merely where gusts worry
dull troughs and avid gleams.

Meaning in point of fact waves
lap-lapping to amuse themselves
while higher levels bide their time.

    *

Fresh out of sympathy cards
things are that bad but easier
than life with no horizon line.

Although most, it is true, persist
who never did master their iCal
and here remain watchful enough.

Except to be honest why bother
every damn thing is wiped off
in the re-sale eventually all of it.

3.

Evening falling well that is still
reliable although no bird tonight
presumes to launch its flight.

The heavenly host instead rises
from fiery beds to speak to me
but I would say that wouldn't I.

Fireflies that is courteous lights
albeit mad dogs in their fashion
frisky through the dusk advance.

*

Call it paradise lost or more like
paradise impossible when claws
scrabble to rip my skylight open.

Also that dry note like cobwebs
coughed into the boiler's throat
on the dot as darkness settles in.

Until hello as usual the future
meets me with low intelligence
in the first two inches of gin.

*

Occasionally an ocean breeze
stinking of fish could be worse
just think of Gorilla Gang turf.

I might also mention there are
green peppers frying in the pan
and notice one losing it to gold.

But come on! That might well be
enough to contemplate in one day
before shutting down entirely.

＊

Avernus which means bird-less
a sulphur lake in all probability
although not here so far as I know.

Here birds doze on black water
or blindly scavenge steered by
piratical scouring of the Earth.

Here my cat sits in the holly bush
with her mouth already wide open
to snaffle wings as they unfold.

＊

My country gods I left behind
my soft approaches also
and my dreams that fly the day.

What hope remains my death
must give and that is not
to exaggerate in the slightest.

Meanwhile I fatten myself up
on forms without their bodies
and if feathers and dust so be it.

ACKNOWLEDGEMENTS AND NOTES

Acknowledgements

The poems in 'Peace Talks' are based on interviews I held with British soldiers and their relatives in spring 2014, mostly in Camp Bad Fallingbostel in Germany. I am grateful to the following: Lance Bombardier Stephen North ('War Debts'); Padre David Anderson and Sharon Anderson ('Fickelty'); Dr Margaret Evison ('The Gardener'). I am also grateful to Melissa Fitzgerald, the producer of the Radio 4 programme *Coming Home*, in which these poems first appeared.

Some of the other poems in *Laurels and Donkeys* are 'found poems' and contain various kinds of collaboration. A few use the words of others without much alteration, others edit and rearrange an existing text, and others combine existing sources with my own words. I gratefully acknowledge the following: for 'Setting the Scene', a letter written by Captain Ted Wilson, quoted in *Weeds* by Richard Mabey (2010); for 'Laurels and Donkeys', *The Old Century* by Siegfried Sassoon (1938); for 'The Life of Harry Patch', *The Last Fighting Tommy* by Harry Patch and Richard Van Emden; for 'The Station at Vitebsk', the Memoirs of Bella Chagall, quoted in *Chagall: Love and Exile* by Jackie Wullschlager (2008); for 'The Minister', *A Visit to Iraq* by Gordon Campbell (unpublished); for 'Losses', *The Good Soldiers* by David Finkell (2009); for 'The Vallon Men', *The Marines of 40 Commando are Back from the Front* by Karen McVeigh, *Guardian*, 18 Nov 2010; for 'The Fence', *Yellow Birds* by Kevin Powers (2012).

I acknowledge the following sources for other poems in this book: for 'Whale Music', *Leviathan* by Philip Hoare (2008); for 'The Conclusion of Joseph Turrill', *An Oxfordshire Market Gardeners*, eds Eve Dawson and Shirley Royal (1993); for 'The Discoveries of Geography', *A History of the World in Twelve Maps* (2013) by Jerry Brotton; for 'The Death of Francesco Borromini', *Borromini* by Anthony Blunt (1979); for 'The White Bear', *Arctic Dreams* by Barry Lopez. 'Hardly a Day' adopts some phrases from John Dryden's translation of *The Aeneid*.

I'm grateful to the editors of the following, in which previously uncollected poems have appeared: *American Scholar*; *Beltway Poetry Quarterly*; *Fusion*; *Interim*; *Liberties*; *New Yorker*; *New York Review of Books*; *Times Literary Supplement*.

Notes

Several of the previously published poems in this book have been revised since their first appearance. Most of these revisions are small; in the case of *Essex Clay*, however, the alterations are much more substantial and designed to create what is in effect a different poem for a different context.

The following is a list of books in which the poems first appeared:

PART ONE: POEMS 1977–2015

1.
'Anne Frank Huis': *Secret Narratives*, 1983; 'Kanpur', 'Tamworth', 'Belfast', 'Look', 'A Blow to the Head', 'Judgement', 'Cutting', 'The Prague Milk Bottle', 'It is an Offence': *Love in a Life*, 1991; 'Serenade', 'The Fox Provides for Himself', 'A Glass of Wine': *Public Property*, 2002; 'The Sin', 'On the Balcony', 'A Dutch Interior', 'Bright Star', 'Raven', 'Passing On', 'The Mower', 'The Cinder Path': *The Cinder Path*, 2009; 'Of All the Birds', 'Are You There?': *The Customs House*, 2012; 'A Fight in Poland', 'Laying the Fire': *Peace Talks*, 2015.

2.
from 'The Exploration of Space': 'Pyongsan', 'Kwangju', 'Montauk', 'Orkney', 'Home Farm', 'Holy Island': *The Customs House, 2012*.

3.

from 'Laurels and Donkeys': 'Setting the Scene', 'Laurels and Donkeys', 'The Life of Harry Patch', 'The Death of Harry Patch', 'The Station at Vitebsk', 'The Korean Memorial at Hiroshima', 'Now Then', 'Demobbed', 'The Minister', 'Losses', 'The Vallon Men' 'Home Front': *The Customs House*, 2012; 'Peace Talks', 'The Fence': *Peace Talks*, 2015; 'Finis', uncollected.

4.

'Mythology', 'Self Help': *Public Property*, 2002; 'London Plane', 'The Customs House', 'Whale Music', 'Hosannah', 'The Death of Francesco Borromini': *The Customs House*, 2012; 'The Realms of Gold', 'The Conclusion of Joseph Turrill', 'The Discoveries of Geography': *Peace Talks*, 2015.

PART TWO: POEMS 2015–2022

1.

'Juliet': from *Essex Clay*, 2018.

2.

'Waders', 'On Her Blindness', 'The Ring', 'In the Family', 'Chincoteague', 'The Bee Tree': uncollected.

3.

'Randomly Moving Particles': *Randomly Moving Particles*, 2020.

4.

'The White Bear', 'What the Grass Says': *Randomly Moving Particles*, 2020; 'Evening Traffic', 'The Catch', 'Among the Others', 'Hardly a Day': uncollected.